REPORTING AMERICA AT WAR

HYPERION

NEW YORK

# REPORTING AMERICA AT WAR

———| AN ORAL HISTORY |———

COMPILED BY

## MICHELLE FERRARI

WITH COMMENTARY BY

## JAMES TOBIN

Library of Congress Cataloging-in-Publication Data

Reporting America at war : an oral history / compiled by Michelle Ferrari with commentary by James Tobin.—1st ed.
    p.   cm.
    Includes index.
    ISBN: 1-4013-0072-3
    1. War—Press coverage—United States—History—20th century.   2. War correspondents—United States—Interviews.   I. Ferrari, Michelle.
II. Tobin, James, 1956–

PN4784.W37R46 2003
070.4'49355—dc21

                                                            2003049966

Hyperion books are available for special promotions and premiums. For details contact Michael Rentas, Manager, Inventory and Premium Sales, Hyperion, 77 West 66th Street, 11th floor, New York, New York 10023, or call 212-456-0133.

FIRST EDITION

10 9 8 7 6 5 4 3 2 1

Book design by Casey Hampton

# CONTENTS

FOREWORD

One day, while working on the documentary film series to which this book is a companion, I was given a stark reminder of precisely why the history of American war correspondence matters. The editorial assistants on the project had just begun to screen and catalog hundreds of hours of footage shot by television crews in the jungles of Vietnam—images of U.S. Marines lighting thatched roofs on fire with Zippo lighters, napalm canisters floating earthward in slow motion before erupting in molten fire, jaded grunts smoking marijuana through the barrel of a shotgun, and everywhere, in frame after frame, reporters commenting on the action. To me, these were familiar images, ones that had first flickered before my adolescent eyes back in the 1970s. But to the assistant editors working with me—men and women a generation younger, whose only exposure to war reporting had come from Grenada, Panama, and Operation Desert Storm—the scenes were both a shock and a revelation. They simply had no idea that American journalists had ever been allowed to report a war so freely. Wartime news, in their experience, came more or less directly from the Pentagon.

What I realized that afternoon was just how much the restrictive press policies of the 1980s and 1990s have minimized our expectations of the media in times of war. As Rick MacArthur, publisher of *Harper's* and author of a fine book about the coverage of the Gulf War, once put it to me: "Americans have lost the habit of expecting to know what the military does in its name." Perhaps, with the Iraq War and the policy of "embedding" journalists now a part of history, this has already begun to change. But I wonder if many of us don't simply accept that the news will never provide us with a complete picture of what takes place on the battlefield.

As the oral histories in this volume make clear, reporting war is a dangerous, complicated, and often imperfect business. The information that makes it back to the home front can depend as much on the predilections of censors and editors and network news directors as it does on the observations and judgment of individual reporters. And regardless of the quality of the journalism, stories about warfare seldom bear any resemblance to the actual lived experience of combat. However, it is equally clear that the way wars are reported has a profound effect on the way they are remembered and understood—and hence, on our ability as citizens to make reasoned judgments about our nation's military actions abroad. "War is the most intimate commitment that the American government can make of its people," Walter Cronkite argues in these pages. "We need to know every detail about how the troops are performing in our name."

As Americans, we should expect nothing less.

*Stephen Ives*
*Director of the PBS series* Reporting America at War
*May 2003*

REPORTING AMERICA AT WAR

# INTRODUCTION

A good line appears on the first page of *My War*, Andy Rooney's memoir of his time as a soldier correspondent for the Army newspaper *Stars and Stripes* in World War II. "If you break your leg and go to a doctor who knows all about broken legs but has never broken his own," Rooney says, "you know just a little bit about broken legs that the doctor does not."

In the matter of war correspondence, I'm like the doctor. I wrote a biography of the World War II reporter Ernie Pyle. But I was born in 1956—too young for Vietnam and too old for anything that came later. I was a newspaper reporter for a long time. But I have never even held a firearm in my hands, much less heard one fired in anger. I've read a lot about war correspondents, especially those of World War II, in the same way that others have read a lot about the Civil War. I find war correspondents interesting. But I don't really know what it's like to be one, and the only time I was offered a chance to find out, I said no without even asking my wife.

If I could have overcome my fear, I would have been like most reporters who can say they once were war correspondents. These are the ones who made a quick trip to a combat zone, did some reporting for a few weeks or months, then went back to their regular jobs for good. A small number have done much more than that, and played a much larger role. They have created a tradition, a genre, and a distinctive body of work. They are remembered and their work is reprinted because they have shaped American perceptions of war—of particular conflicts and of war in general. Those perceptions, in turn, are the ground on which we make many of our most important decisions as a nation. What we think about war matters deeply, so the people who tell us about war matter deeply, too.

Fourteen important war correspondents are represented here, mostly in their own words, thanks to Stephen Ives, Michelle Ferrari, and their colleagues at Insignia Films. With the backing of the National Endowment for the Humanities and the Corporation for Public Broadcasting, these filmmakers set out to tell the story of American war correspondence. They began their work in the late 1990s, a time of peace in the United States. It was an important endeavor then and it is more important now, as the country finds itself in a new age of war and rumors of war, a frightening era as different from the 1990s as the 1930s and '40s were from the 1920s.

The filmmakers recorded extraordinary interviews with great war correspondents and people who have known them well. But films can only be so long, with time enough for only fractions of the full interviews. Ives and Ferrari wanted readers to hear more from these remarkable men and women—hence, their decision to publish an oral history in the form of a book. As a historian, I'm grateful to them for doing so. As an anxious citizen of the United States in a new time of trouble, I urge others to read what these journalists have to say.

. . .

War journalism is better understood when one knows a little about the conditions in which it's created. I'm not talking about "writing from the foxholes," a heroic fiction that reporters themselves have spread around. Ernie Pyle himself, who became famous and popular as the chronicler of soldiers' daily lives in World War II, wrote a story in a foxhole exactly once. Sometimes war correspondents are in danger. Mostly they're not. They seldom find themselves in the middle of an actual clash of arms, and when they do, it's more often by accident than by intent. Mostly they talk to guys who were in the battle after it's over, if their "access" is good, or to officers up the ladder, if their access is less good, or to military PIOs—public information officers—who don't go into battles at all. If they need to write something, they go back to the press camp or the hotel, where they can send the story to their editors.

With the exception of a few truly daring or obsessed individuals, the difficulty for most war reporters is not physical danger. It's finding something their editors might want, gathering sufficient facts and quotes to make a story, and getting the story written and transmitted to their home office on deadline. This describes the life of all daily journalists, of course, but it's worse for reporters on foreign soil, in the confusion of war. They work under great time pressure and in a ferment of disorganization, even desperation. One of the reasons we reprint and admire the work of such war writers as Pyle, A. J. Liebling of the *New Yorker*, Martha Gellhorn, and the Vietnam-era freelancer Michael Herr is that they didn't write under the pressure of a daily deadline. They had a little more time than their "daily" colleagues to chat, reflect, and revise. But even with more time, war reporters cannot see the future. They lack the historian's advantage of hindsight to know which war will seem just and wise, or at least necessary, and which will seem misguided and wasteful. They can't write whatever they want. They work for editors, who in turn are producing a commodity for sale to an audience, which has its own tastes and preferences. They are either censored by the military or denied access to things they want to see. All war journalism, the trivial and the lasting, is cooked up in this high-pressure oven of conflicting claims and restrictions. The reporter's lines of vision are always limited. It has always been so and will remain so.

Many of the things that drive people nuts about the media, including most of the errors they make, are not the result of conspiracy or bias. They are the result of having to do everything in a terrible rush. Reporters make phone calls in a rush; conduct interviews in a rush; write and edit stories in a rush. Even their thinking is done in a rush, with little time—no time at all, usually—for background reading or a quiet effort to think something through. Quick thinking means relying on clichés—not just clichés of expression, but what the great *Boston Globe* editor and writing coach Donald Murray has called "clichés of vision," the stereotyped ways of seeing reality that lead to formulaic and ultimately empty journalism. I think clichés of vision have led to many more distortions of reality than official censorship.

Thinking and writing under pressure require journalists to divide reality into categories that are sometimes laughably simple. But the categories have served their purpose since war correspondence as we know it began, shortly before the American Civil War, and they will stay with us for the foreseeable future.

The first category is called simply "news," or "hard news." Most war reporting has fallen into this category. These are the stories that answer the questions "Are we winning?" "Are we losing?" and "What happened yesterday?" Readers scan them and never look at them again. To write these stories, journalists have to rely on information given out by the military, which is the only organization in a war zone with the means of gathering information about the overall military campaigns and pound it into a sensible shape. Even the most powerful news organizations have nothing like that kind of information-gathering apparatus in war. We speak of several hundred reporters in the Persian Gulf conflicts as if it were a huge number. In fact, it would be pitifully inadequate if the news organizations themselves had to find out how the war was really going. No single reporter can give the hard news on a day's worth of war. Morley Safer of CBS News held his hands in front of him, bracketing a segment of space two feet wide, and said: "A reporter sees this much of the war at any given moment." So the journalists assigned to write the "hard news lead" about the war on any particular day—"The Overview," as the *New York Times* calls it—have no choice but to rely heavily on what the military tells them. If, on that day, the military is covering its ass more than telling the truth, the quality of the news will suffer.

The second category of reality in the news business goes by the name "feature," "soft news," or "color," as in the "colorful" details of war that are gathered and packaged mostly in "sidebars" to compensate for the awful tedium of military press briefings. These stories answer one question: "What is war like?" A single war correspondent *can* answer this one, and most of the war stories we revere are stories that do so. Several journalists in this book built their careers on the question. It takes various forms, depending on who's asking.

What is war like for the infantry soldier, the pilot, the sailor, the supply sergeant? Ernie Pyle specialized in this territory. It is the question that people at home ask most urgently, especially those who have sent sons and daughters to fight. Ward Just, Morley Safer, and Gloria Emerson did great work here, too, though they were less reassuring than Pyle.

What is war like for the enemy, or for the civilian whose home is bombed by accident or negligence, or the mother whose child was maimed or killed? Martha Gellhorn and Christiane Amanpour have answered this variant of the question with deeply disturbing results. Peter Arnett caused a furor and was called a traitor for trying to answer it for CNN in Baghdad in 1991.

What does war look and sound and smell like? Edward R. Murrow is remembered most for working on this.

A few gifted reporters, several of whom speak in this volume, have ignored the artificial barrier between the hard and soft halves of the reporter's reality. Still confined to their one small section of war—"the worm's-eye view," Pyle called it—they have probed that section for all it can reveal, not only to show what war is like, but to pose difficult variants of the hard-news question: How is the war going? They may ask: What is the cost of this war, in blood, treasure, and trouble, and is the cost worth the prize? They may explore an isolated, hard-news aspect of the war that illuminates the whole. In Vietnam, Neil Sheehan and David Halberstam did this in their reports of the Battle of Ap Bac, where the strange behavior of South Vietnamese soldiers called into question the very premises of the American Mission. A classic example occurred when Homer Bigart wrote of an event that other reporters no doubt dismissed as unworthy of coverage. To control malaria in Vietnam's central lowlands, Americans had sprayed villagers' huts with the insecticide DDT to kill the local mosquitos. It killed the local cats as well. With the cats gone, the rat population surged, and the rats laid waste to the rich Vietnamese rice crop. The government of South Vietnam, already fighting Communist claims that it had done nothing to help farmers, responded ineffectually, and the United States had to scramble to import and distribute many tons of rat poison. In a story of fewer than five hundred words in the New York Times—which began, "American DDT spray killed the cats that ate the rats that devoured the crops..."—Bigart put his finger on a small but telling symbol of what Americans were getting themselves into.

Not many reporters are blessed with Bigart's penetrating intelligence or Pyle's lovely prose style or Chris Hedges's tragic insight. But any hardworking reporter can look carefully at what he sees, ask questions, and report what he finds out. Anyone can compare what people do to what they say, tell the truth as he sees it, and call attention to lies. Even on deadline.

Sometimes the truth runs counter to the purpose of the soldiers who accommodate reporters in the war zone. When leaders, soldiers, reporters, and the public agree the purpose is worthy, and that violence in pursuit of the purpose is justified, as in World War II, then the soldiers and the reporters get along pretty well. When there is disagreement about ends and means, and about who's telling the truth about them, then there will be trouble.

The leading example—so far—is Vietnam. There, from an early point, reporters pointed out that U.S. officials and soldiers were not fulfilling the aims of U.S. policy. They were asking and answering the hard-news question "How's the war going?" The answer was, "Not too well; better do something about it." As the years passed, some in the Vietnam press corps began to say the avowed policy itself—to help the South Vietnamese govern themselves—was doomed to failure, or that the terrible means were so out of proportion to the dubious ends that the war had become simply stupid and cruel.

For this, the military brass—not so much the working soldiers—accused reporters of failing to be "on the team," as Pyle and his comrades supposedly had been in World War II. That accusation has echoed down through the years, with the Pentagon of 2002 warily keeping reporters away from the action in Afghanistan for fear they, too, will betray "the team." When Pentagon planners allowed reporters to be "embedded" in the military units that invaded Iraq early in 2003, they took a giant step away from the press-wary policies of the post-Vietnam era. The new policy is promising. But it makes enormous demands on the press and the military alike. "Embedded" reporters (an unfortunate coinage, to be sure) must resist the temptation to identify too closely with their soldier hosts—to become mere cheerleaders. And the brass must stick to the policy even when soldiers in the field tell the reporters hard truths that deviate from the Pentagon's official line. If both sides behave as they should, then the decision to allow reporters to do their jobs will serve everyone well—the soldiers; the public; later generations, who will have an independent record of the war; even innocent civilians in Iraq. In the long run, truth is always healthier than fiction.

Even when the truth turns painful, I hope no one will say again that reporters who tell the truth are not "on the team." Honest reporters are no less patriotic than those who cheer the military no matter what it does. Pyle and Halberstam, Gellhorn and Hedges, all have been squarely "on the team" in the sense that they wanted what was best for their country, and perhaps for others, too.

It's equally wrongheaded for critics of the press to say reporters have been "willing propagandists" when they covered a war from their own side of the lines. In fact, every reporter is a citizen of somewhere and a believer in something. Everyone is on some team or another. Even pacifists constitute a team, with its own values and point of view. The question is which team to choose, not whether one is on or off. The novelist Ward Just, a war correspondent for the *Washington Post* long ago, once put this quite beautifully: "The best and most faithful of these characters come to understand that in some profound sense they are owned by their memories, and that in turn their own angle of vision—in essence, whether they see themselves as insider or outsider, paleface or redskin—depends on the earliest circumstances of their own lives, their childhood fears and joys, and on how danger was defined..."

There is a lot of talk in journalism classes and conferences, even in this book, about good war journalism as a bulwark of democracy—that people in democratic nations have a special right to know how wars are being fought on their behalf, especially if their sons and daughters are doing the fighting. This is indisputable, and an essential reason to demand much from war correspondents and the military organizations that accommodate them.

So war journalism is democratic journalism. But often it is also what the magazine editor Bill Buford, who has published some, calls "voyeuristic travel writing." It attempts to satisfy a fascination with war that many feel, including me. We don't like to admit it. Honest reporters do. Pyle often referred to the appeal of war—the aesthetic appreciation one feels in the face of a terrible spectacle; the comradeship that grows out of shared struggle; the sense that one is living and seeing life at its most intense. These things, too, propel reporters toward war zones. War is always the biggest story in any newsroom. Fascination, not democracy, explains that. So this, too, is part of the context in which war journalism is created.

The chapters that follow are composed of words spoken aloud in interviews with the Insignia Films team. This is not a history of war correspondence, but a series of conversations *about* that history with people who helped to make it, or who saw it made. The book runs in rough chronological order, from Edward R. Murrow to Christiane Amanpour. In the case of three deceased writers—Murrow, Martha Gellhorn, and Homer Bigart—the chapters contain the comments of associates and friends.

One has to read what the journalists actually wrote to appreciate them fully and to learn from them, so each chapter concludes with references to published collections of the correspondent's writings, in some cases to biographies or memoirs. Samples of the work of Edward R. Murrow, Martha Gellhorn, Homer Bigart, Malcolm W. Browne, David Halberstam, Peter Arnett, Ward Just, Gloria Emerson, and dozens of other American war correspondents appear in two superb collections published by the Library of America. These are *Reporting World War II*, volume 1 (1938–1944) and volume 2 (1944–1946), and *Reporting Vietnam*, volume 1 (1959–1969) and volume 2 (1969–1975).

*James Tobin*
*March 2003*

# EDWARD R. MURROW

## WORLD WAR II

*Edward R. Murrow's career roughly marks the beginning of our own era of war correspondence. Before his time, Americans had depended solely on the printed word to learn about their wars. Readers of the 1860s and 1890s had been afforded heavy coverage of the Civil War and the Spanish-American War. But faulty communications facilities often caused long delays. And journalists who substituted lurid imagination for diligent reporting often fostered distortions. In World War I, coverage of the eighteen-month U.S. intervention was hampered by censors and heavily salted with government propaganda. Indeed, American isolationism of the interwar period was in part the angry response of a people who felt they had been lied to about the Great War in Europe.*

*With the approach of World War II, American coverage of war became more sophisticated, more immediate, and more dependable. Various factors were responsible, including the growing appetite among educated readers for solid information about the new world crisis; the expanding influence of such great newspapers as the* New York Times *and the* New York Herald Tribune; *and better communications facilities. Edward R. Murrow, the first great news broadcaster, was also part of the change. Before he entered Americans' consciousness as a deep voice saying, "This...is London," radio broadcasting about public affairs had been a tepid business of airing speeches or reading a few headlines. But as Stanley Cloud and Lynne Olson put it in* The Murrow Boys, *he and his colleagues at midcentury essentially "invented broadcast journalism." They introduced a startling new sense of immediacy and authenticity to journalism, and it could be argued that Murrow's on-the-scene reporting forced print correspondents to make their own writing more accurate and more descriptive.*

*To cover events live, with sound and later pictures as accompaniments, was Murrow's innovation more than anyone else's, and the organization he built during the war established standards and models for broadcasting that remain influential. Murrow also hired or shaped the careers of numerous broadcast journalists who became major figures in their own right, including Eric Sevareid, William L. Shirer, Charles Collingwood, Howard K. Smith, and Daniel Schorr.*

*Murrow is remembered here by Walter Cronkite, who turned down Murrow's job offer at the end of World War II but joined him at CBS later, and by two of the younger members of Murrow's wartime staff. One is Larry LeSueur, whom Murrow hired in London the week before the German invasion of Poland in September 1939. He became the first reporter to broadcast the news—uncensored and unauthorized—of the liberation of Paris five years later. The other, Richard C. Hottelet, had worked for the U.S. Office of War Information (OWI), an agency established by executive order in June 1942 to serve as a liaison between the press and the federal government, and to disseminate in-*

*formation at home and abroad. Later, as a member of Murrow's staff, Hottelet was the first reporter to broadcast from the Battle of the Bulge. Both were influential figures at CBS for many years.*

———

RICHARD C. HOTTELET: I had been in London for OWI, doing propaganda to occupied Europe—leaflets dropped by airplanes, radio broadcasts—and I had been in North Africa doing leaflet stuff for the British Army. I got back to London and found there had been a shake-up of OWI in Washington. Some people came in who didn't seem to promise much fun, and I decided to leave. I went to Ed Murrow and said, "Here I am, do you have a job?" And he said, "Well, maybe," and he checked with New York and very soon he called me up and said, "You've got a job."

Murrow was a remarkable man. He was very serious. He had a no-nonsense delivery and appeared somewhat saturnine. But he wasn't dark at all in his character. I mean, when he smiled, it was like the sun coming through clouds. But he once told me he had never learned to play. He had grown up poor and made his own way. He had, I think, a drive which few people have. His background was ordinary working-class. He had dealt with people in real terms, so reality was his hallmark, and the metaphors he used and the images he made were images that people like him and like nine-tenths of the human race could understand.

———

*Murrow had been born on his parents' farm in Polecat Creek, North Carolina. When he was five years old, the family moved to the Pacific Northwest, where he lumberjacked to help pay his way through Washington State College. Winning high grades as a speech major, he considered a career in college teaching. But his ambition took him to New York, where he landed a job at CBS. In 1937 the network sent him to London to arrange broadcasts of educational talks and light entertain-*

*ment—children's choir concerts and the like. He hoped to broadcast reports on the growing world crisis. But his superiors in New York told him to shoot for the standard CBS had set in 1932, when it produced a live broadcast of an English nightingale in song. (One CBS executive called this "the greatest thing this company has ever done for Anglo-American relations.") Newspaper correspondents held broadcasters in such low esteem that they refused Murrow's application to join the American Foreign Correspondents' Association in London.*

*But Murrow and his first hire, the highly regarded print reporter William Shirer, soon had a story their superiors in New York could not refuse—Hitler's bloodless conquests of Austria and Czechoslovakia, and the deepening likelihood of a second world war. When the war came and the Germans attacked Great Britain by air in 1940, Murrow and his growing staff covered the raids live from London's rooftops, and Murrow's voice became as well known in the United States as President Roosevelt's. He went on to cover many key moments in the war, including air raids over occupied Europe and the liberation of Buchenwald. Later, he became equally influential in the early years of television news.*

*Walter Cronkite was working as a wire-service reporter for United Press in the United States when Murrow did his broadcasts during the London Blitz.*

———

WALTER CRONKITE: He brought home the real horror of this bombing. We didn't have instantaneous film in those days, of course. We had the newsreels that would show up in the movie houses eventually, but in lieu of that, [we had] the word pictures that he drew of the horror of these all-night bombings, the people in air-raid shelters, the disaster above the surface. It had an immense impact on the American public. Nobody had covered a war quite like that. There had been some coverage of the preliminaries—the war in

Ethiopia, for instance. But this was obviously the big one—this great capital to which Americans had some affinity.

RICHARD C. HOTTELET: He was driven to tell people in the United States what was going on in Europe—the growth of Hitler to the dimensions of a world threat. He dealt with it eloquently, factually, coldly, but with an inner flame.

Murrow's great original contribution was to invent broadcast news from abroad. Before that, in the '30s, broadcast news was somebody ripping wire copy off a teleprinter and reading it through a microphone. But Murrow wanted to report in the field, and to hire people who were reporters. That had never been done before.

No one was hired because he was good-looking or had a beautiful voice. We were all working reporters, street reporters. Putting that on the air and making the content of the story the main point—not the technique, and no charm about it—that was his contribution. There were no histrionics, no tricks.

WALTER CRONKITE: He was not trained as a journalist. He didn't have any practice broadcasting or covering news. He just did it instinctively, and, of course, he did it exceedingly well. He obviously was a very intelligent man, a very well-educated man, and he had a natural curiosity, a natural concern about the world around him and the people around him. He could respond as an average man might to the stimulus of the moment, but also approach it with an intelligent, analytical turn.

His voice carried authority, which is very important.

LARRY LESUEUR: He was conscious of voice, and very few people had been trained as well as he had in voice and enunciation. He didn't seem to search for words, and he wasn't as hampered as the rest of us were by newspaper training, because he didn't care about leads—who, when, why, where. He was a writer. He couldn't even type in those days—he would use the hunt-and-peck system—but he managed to put down words that were almost imagery, that connoted by his tones the emotions he wished to arouse in people. We didn't realize—I don't think *he* did—how much his voice had to do with his broadcasting. He had a baritone voice, and he knew the powers of silence. He would say, "Good evening. This...is London." He knew the power of punctuation, which nobody else realized.

All I thought of [while broadcasting] was talking to the person [in the broadcast studio] who had just said to me, "Go ahead." I didn't realize how much power I had to evoke images. Ed Murrow did, I think. He evoked emotion in his voice and his choice of language. It was almost biblical, because his mother had read the Bible to his two brothers and him as boys, growing up.

RICHARD C. HOTTELET: When he was at the microphone doing his news broadcasts, the sweat would come down his face and it would concentrate on his chin. He had one leg on the ball of his foot and it would bob up and down. He was there; he was physically engaged.

LARRY LESUEUR: To Murrow, every broadcast he did was his last broadcast. He had almost inconceivable powers of concentration. He would not hear anything that interfered with his trying to concentrate on his words.

I know that I became inured to the sight of death, both in London and after D Day. But he was always very, very sensitive to the deprivations and suffering of the people, so much so that it took a toll on him. But the more tired he would get, the better he thought. He was full of admiration for the people of London. He saw what suffering they were undergoing, and I think it grew on him.

It didn't make any difference to Murrow whether he was first with a story or not. When we first overran the concentration camps [in 1945], he went over there a couple of weeks later, and his descriptions of the concentration camps are living today. He didn't have to be first.

RICHARD C. HOTTELET: I think Murrow was a born leader. He didn't push people, didn't order them, but we all followed him. He never gave an assignment that he wouldn't give himself. I remember some of the broadcasts we did from London. He would always be the first to go up on the roof and see where the action was that night. As a matter of fact, he did things himself that he might not have given as an assignment. His bombing trips with the RAF [Royal Air Force] went deep into Germany. We knew that he was the bravest of the lot, and that was part of the respect in which he was held.

He was an eminently fair man—no favorites. His treatment of me was, "Well, you're a journalist; go and do your job." He never gave me any lessons in broadcasting or told me how to do something or what not to do. But he followed the product very carefully. I remember I was out on some airfield and I came back and did a piece on it, and I said, "I didn't know whether the weather was going to be good or whether it was going to be bad." And he said, "You dealt with the weather pretty expansively." So he knew what was going on. But he never said, "You shouldn't have said it this way," or, "You should have said it that way." Once he had hired you, you had complete freedom.

Murrow was in everything up to his ears. When he was almost speechless at Buchenwald, it was because Buchenwald had taken him over. When he was in Vienna at the time of the *Anschluss* [Hitler's takeover of Austria], he absorbed what was going on. He wasn't talking through a pane of glass—a sort of sanitized, distant experience. He was in it. It was part of him.

He knew and loved the language, and dealt with it carefully and eloquently. I have a feeling he was influenced very much by Winston Churchill. Sometimes, when he spoke, and perhaps more often when he broadcast, there was a Churchillian flavor to his language.

Murrow was convivial, too, and informal. So he was a complex man, a many-faceted man. But all of it was real. There was never anything put on. He didn't try to impress anyone or to persuade anyone, particularly. He said what he had to say. He said it the best way he could, and if you didn't take it, you didn't take it. But if you took it, you were ahead of the game.

FOR FURTHER READING:

Joseph Persico, *Edward R. Murrow: An American Original* (McGraw-Hill, 1988)

A. M. Sperber, *Murrow: His Life and Times* (Freundlich Books, 1988)

Stanley Cloud and Lynne Olson, *The Murrow Boys: Pioneers on the Front Lines of Broadcast Journalism* (Houghton Mifflin, 1996)

# WALTER CRONKITE

## WORLD WAR II · VIETNAM

*Walter Cronkite, anchor of* CBS Evening News *from 1962 to 1981, was the most visible journalist of his generation and one of the most highly regarded—a figure whose aura of fairness and calm lent a measure of steadiness to a time of upheaval. His career and reputation were built on the foundation of his years as a print correspondent for United Press in World War II, during which he covered as many campaigns as perhaps any other reporter. This is a transcript of a recorded interview.*

With Pearl Harbor, I wanted to get into the war as a correspondent right away. I was working for United Press in New York, and I said, "I want to go." The first assignment that came up was the Navy in the Atlantic, and they said, "There you go" and that was it. I never looked back. I never thought about being a soldier after that. I could do far more as a correspondent than [as] an infantryman. There was no criticism of that. We were out there with the guys in the foxholes, in the airplanes, in the parachute jump groups, in the gliders. It was entirely voluntary, and the frequently asked question to the reporters from G.I.s was, "What the hell are you doing here? Do you have to be here?" "No," we'd say, "we don't have to be." "Well, my God, why are you here, then?" They looked upon us as heroes, in a way, as we looked upon them.

We didn't stay on one beat during the entire war. We all did several things. For instance, I was one of the first correspondents to get credentials to cover the Navy after Pearl Harbor—the Atlantic Fleet, that is. I went off on the Atlantic Fleet convoys, and was still doing that when we made the invasion into North Africa [in October 1942], so I went along to cover that. United Press had me return to England, where I covered the air war. That was the principal story until D Day [June 6, 1944]. Shortly after D Day, I was recalled to England to prepare for the 101st Airborne landing in Holland. I was covering the British First Army in the Netherlands when the Battle of the Bulge began, so suddenly I was in the Battle of the Bulge. They just moved me wherever I was needed at the moment, as they did with most of the other reporters. Where was there a hole? What was happening? They'd send you your marching orders to get going to another assignment. You could request [an assignment], and if they thought it was a good match, they might send you along. That was part of the game as well.

We were assigned by our companies to armies. They'd say, "Want you to cover the Third Army" and you'd find out where Third Army headquarters were and you'd become a member of the press camp. The press had quarters set up somewhere around the Army headquarters, and we had briefings by the officers. Then, after a [daily] briefing on where the action was going to be, if the action was one we wanted to see and then report on, we would get a jeep

assignment—usually the same jeep each day—and we'd pi
our jeep and go off to the front. They gave us a chart and
to locate the group we wanted to find, and we found them
tually through the help of the military police on the roads. We'd
hunker down with them for the day or a couple of days or more
while that particular battle engagement went on.

———

*The job of a front-line correspondent in World War II was harried
and difficult. Most reporters worked under intense deadline pressure,
filing at least one story and often more every day. Those, like Cronkite,
who worked for the press associations—United Press, Associated Press,
Reuters—might file a news overview, then another news story plus a
feature, all in a single day.*

———

[The day's stories] would depend entirely on the action. It might
very well be a feature story of some bravery that I witnessed or
heard about, or it would be the difficulty or success a unit might
have had in action. The unit might be as small as a platoon and
could be as large as a brigade; it was just whatever was going on.

We were right with the soldiers—no problem with access whatsoever. We talked to them; they talked to us, G.I.s and officers alike.
The military did not make any attempt to monitor the interviews
we got with the men. There was nothing like we had in the [Persian]
Gulf War [in 1991], where they had a senior officer standing by
whenever we talked to a G.I. or an officer.

In the evening we got back to press camp and wrote the story.
We had to file it with the intelligence officer for whatever unit we
were with. Then that went to the Army G-2 [intelligence] officer,
and he would pass it for transmission, or sometimes make deletions
and changes. The copy was passed back to us to see whether we
wanted to transmit it that way. If we didn't want to transmit it that

way, we could argue about it. Sometimes we won and sometimes we lost. The copy sometimes was held up in London; the top G-2 would spike it. But we were advised that it was spiked and it would be held until it could be released. For instance, if there was something about losses and they didn't want to reveal that for the next two or three days, they'd hold it three days and then release it. If it was new equipment being committed to battle, which happened with the Air Force more than once, they might want to hold it for weeks. But eventually they would release it.

———

*Censorship rules varied from theater to theater, service branch to service branch, even censor to censor. The popular columnist Ernie Pyle, for example, was permitted to publish columns that criticized U.S. officials for tolerating Vichy French officials in North Africa in 1943. But a year later Pyle was prevented from publishing an account of U.S. soldiers suffering from combat fatigue, or "shell shock." Yet Cronkite wrote similar stories that were passed.*

———

[Censorship] would begin with a simple statement: "You can't print that!" Then you'd find out why. There were certain things we knew weren't going to pass. We tried to get by with them because we were trying to report everything we could. But casualties, for instance—they weren't anxious to let the enemy know how successful they had been in any given action, how many lives they'd claimed, how much matériel they'd destroyed, the disposition of forces, where the various forces were and what they were equipped with, what kind of vehicles they had, what kind of guns they had. All that kind of thing was pretty much always held up. We could write around it, which we did. We could say that losses were heavy or losses were light. We just couldn't give specifics.

I didn't run into censorship [on stories of servicemen suffering battle fatigue]. But I was writing that kind of story mostly during the air war, so I had the benefit of working with the chief censor in London, and that was a very intelligent operation. Those were mostly lawyers who were rounded up and put into that job. They were not military men by instinct and they had an understanding of protecting the public's right to know.

———

*Sometimes the correspondent had to wrestle with his own ambivalence about exposing himself to danger. Cronkite described such a moment in December 1944, when, in a last attempt to turn the tide against the Allies, German forces launched a massive surprise attack through the dense Ardennes forest in Belgium. Their thrust became known as "the Bulge." For a time, elements of the U.S. First Army were surrounded at the town of Bastogne.*

———

There was a shambles when the Battle of the Bulge started. The UP sent me a crazy cable, which I kept because it said, "We've lost touch with First Army—see if you can get out there and pull this story together." Nobody could pull it together. The intelligence people couldn't pull it together.

I went up to an armored unit because they were most likely to break through to Bastogne. I wanted to find out, obviously, what they were doing, what success they were having. When I got there, a couple of them had just gotten back [from Bastogne] by jeep. It was not safe, by any means, but they'd found a route up there and back. Just about that time, General [Maxwell] Taylor [commander of the 101st Airborne Division, later military adviser to Presidents John F. Kennedy and Lyndon B. Johnson] showed up by jeep. He had just gotten back from the States and was still in his street uniform. He went into headquarters and got a briefing, and when he came out, he said, "Cronkite! You want to go with us?"

clination was to go. When the hell do you get the chance

Bastogne? But then I thought about that trip and the like-

y were going to run into trouble. Also, a second problem arose in my mind. I think it did. I'm not sure. I don't know whether this is justification for cowardice. But as I try to remember it now, I had no way to get the story out of Bastogne. There was no communication out. And here I had a pretty damn good story about having made contact to Bastogne that nobody else had. I had a story that contact could be made, and I also had a story that Taylor was on his way in. And I decided that was better than taking a chance on going up there, a chance of not making it up, and even if I did get up there, of not being able to file the story. But I'm not sure of that; I'm not sure that a little yellow streak didn't appear.

----

*His account brings to mind a comment once made by Robert Capa, who, among his credits as one of the great war photographers, shot the only pictures of U.S. soldiers coming ashore at Normandy's Omaha Beach on D Day in 1944. Capa said: "The war correspondent gets more drinks, more girls, better pay and greater freedom than the soldier, but...having the freedom to choose his spot and being allowed to be a coward and not be executed for it is his torture. The war correspondent has his stake—his life—in his own hands, and he can put it on this horse or that horse, or he can put it back in his pocket at the very last minute."*

----

You went to morning briefings at Third Army, for instance, and they told you about two or three actions taking place that day, and you had to make up your mind where you wanted to go, if you wanted to go at all. Many days, guys, including me, would simply say, "Well, I don't see anything very different in that story. Why should I go up and get my ass shot off for another platoon action?"

That went on all the time, every day. You could turn aro͏ say, "I'm not going to the front today. I don't like what's ͏ today and I'm not gonna go." Of course, if you didn't g͏ ͏͏ enough, your company presumably would recall you. That's not the kind of war correspondent you want at the front.

———

*After World War II, Cronkite covered the Nuremberg war crimes trials and became United Press's bureau chief in Moscow in the early years of the Cold War. In 1950 he joined CBS in the pioneer days of television news, and in 1962 he was named anchorman of* CBS Evening News, *a fifteen-minute broadcast that expanded to thirty minutes in 1963, shortly before the assassination of President John F. Kennedy. Cronkite became a kind of national father figure, a symbol of dependability and fairness. Polls of the late 1960s showed he was "the most trusted man in America." That reputation soon entered the political calculus of a president as public opinion split over the war in Vietnam.*

———

When I first went to Vietnam, in the early stages of our commitment, I was for it. The South Vietnamese regime was at no time a democracy, but we were trying to preserve a fertile ground for democracy in a Southeast Asia that was almost totally Communist. So I thought sending military advisers was a good idea. As we built up those forces and took over the war, I lost my enthusiasm for our presence there.

When I first got there, I was rather upset with our correspondents. It seemed to me there was kind of a juvenile attitude toward the five o'clock briefing [the daily military briefing given to reporters by the U.S. Mission], which was called the "Five O'Clock Follies." After I was there for a while, I learned there was some pretty good cause for that. The story as it was being told by the briefing officers was contradictory to what the correspondents were finding out in the field with the troops. But at the same time, there seemed to be a sort of a challenge game going on in those briefings by the younger correspondents, who hadn't been in war circumstances before, to see who could be the nastiest to the briefing officer, to show the greatest cynicism. It was kind of a derby of cynicism.

———

*As the U.S. military presence expanded enormously, the administration of President Lyndon Johnson issued optimistic forecasts of imminent victory against the Communist regime of North Vietnam and its guerrilla allies, the Vietcong. Then, shortly after General William Westmoreland, commander of U.S. forces, announced that "a sense of despair" was spreading among the enemy, the Communist insurgents mounted a massive and largely unexpected offensive against cities throughout South Vietnam, even penetrating the grounds of the U.S. embassy in the capital, Saigon. The attack began with the Vietnamese New Year, Tet.*

———

When the Tet Offensive came along, it seemed to be a watershed event. We had been told by the military we were winning this war. We were getting all the equivalents of "get the troops out of the trenches by Christmas," "a light at the end of the tunnel," all this sort of thing. And here, suddenly, the Vietcong and the North Vietnamese showed they had the strength to mount a disastrous offensive. There was now a real crisis of American confidence in what we were doing out there. What was the truth? What the devil was happening? My gosh, we're told by the government that we're winning, and then we see this kind of thing, Communist troops even in the streets of Saigon, for heaven's sakes. What's happening? And people really didn't have an answer.

I said, "Why don't we go out and try to answer that question the best we can? Take somebody who hasn't been on the ground

all the time and try to do an impartial job." I would g\
report on the offensive and then, at the conclusion, do a d\
tary. And that's what we did. Dick Salant was the president\
and a very straitlaced guy on any kind of opinion in our \
casting. But he agreed that maybe it was time to step out of the
impartial role and say what I thought about the war. It would be
quite a departure, and we knew there were great dangers in doing
it, but we agreed it should be done, not knowing what I'd find. I
did not know what the conclusion would be when I got out there.
When I came back, I separated completely what I said [in a com-
mentary] from the report we'd just given. I said: "After these words
from sponsors, I will be back with a personal opinion," and I delivered it as such.

———

*In that commentary, delivered on February 27, 1968, Cronkite said it
seemed "more certain than ever that the bloody experience of Vietnam
is to end in a stalemate." Lyndon Johnson was preparing for the 1968
presidential campaign but facing severe criticism, and he regarded
Cronkite's verdict as one more blow to his chances for reelection. A
month later, he announced he would not run.*

———

We got reaction from the White House on a lot of things. Many
nights the president himself would be on the phone. Other nights
people from the White House staff would call and say, "You know,
there're some people around here who think..." You knew who "the
people" around there were! But we didn't hear from anybody on this
one. Months later, Bill Moyers or George Christian [press aides of
Johnson], who'd been there at the moment, told me that the president snapped off CBS after I'd done my little piece and said, "Well,
if I've lost Cronkite, I've lost Middle America." And it was shortly
after that that he announced he was not going to run again.

I think what I had to say was only a small straw on the camel's back, and the camel already was down belly deep in the sand.

They should have had censorship in Vietnam. I believe there should be censorship in wartime. I believe it absolutely firmly. I'm more comfortable when we are clear that our reporting is not putting our troops in jeopardy and making the job more difficult and prolonging the killing. I also understand that the military, in exercising that censorship, definitely needs a civilian appeals court—civilian-trained individuals [who would] understand the right of the people to know.

The point is that in any war situation, this is the most intimate commitment that the American government can make of its people. This is our war, our troops, our boys, our girls. We need to know every detail about how they are performing in our name, both when they perform well and when they perform badly. It's most important when they perform badly, as a matter of fact. So war should be covered intimately. Correspondents should be with the troops everywhere the troops are, in the air, on the ground, under the seas, wherever. Correspondents should be there reporting on it. Their dispatches should go through a censorship procedure so that no military secrets are given to the enemy. But there is the report; it is there for history. It may not be released by censorship immediately, maybe not the next day, maybe not the next month, but it'll be there next year. It'll be there ten years from now.

Today we have no independent film of the [1991] Persian Gulf War—none—because our correspondents, our film crews, were not permitted to go out on the front with the troops. They should have been. The tape they shot should have been sent back to censorship. If it couldn't be released immediately, at least it would be held for eventual release and for history. We don't have that history now. That history is lost to us. It's a crime against the democracy.

———

*At various points during and after the Vietnam conflict, military of-*
*ficials accused reporters of betraying the U.S. cause there, of failing to*
*be "on the team," as correpondents were said to have been during World*
*War II. At the other end of the political spectrum, critics have faulted*
*the World War II press corps for being too enthusiastically "on the*
*team," of failing to serve as watchdog.*

———

In World War II everybody was on the team. We knew what
we were fighting. We knew what the record of the enemy was. We
were perfectly aware of the nature of the fight. In Vietnam, it was
never explained thoroughly what we were doing there. And the
resistance here at home, the divided nation, created a demand for
the kind of coverage we gave, showing them this was a pretty
messed-up war. I don't think there was either a pledge of loyalty in
World War II or a disdain of loyalty or patriotism in Vietnam. It
was just the circumstances of the battles themselves. We were fighting a war in Vietnam, don't forget, that we had no experience of,
as an army or as reporters. And we didn't have any headquarters
we could cover; we had to get out in the jungle with the guys. It
was a vastly different kind of combat.

[The antagonism between the press and the military that began
in Vietnam] created a serious situation which I'm not sure has been
ameliorated completely yet, all these years later. There are some in
the military who claim that the press, particularly television, lost
the war in Vietnam. There was actually a study of this made at the
Pentagon, and that study, which was supposedly impartial, came up
with the fact that the press had not "lost the war in Vietnam," and
that this shibboleth should be put to an end. Of course, you don't
put an end to that sort of thing if there's a feeling of that kind
among the military. And there was such a feeling—very deep—that

if we had supported the war more, if we had not reported some of the things that our correspondents were seeing out there, maybe they could have held on long enough to win. The result of that was to shut the press out of future military ventures.

The next was the invasion of Grenada [in 1983], and there were no correspondents at all involved. None were told about it in advance. None were solicited to go, even under a form of censorship. And when they attempted to get there on their own, they were threatened with being shot by the military.

[The war correspondent's perspective] is no more unique than the perspective of reporters on the beat anywhere—the intimacy of being a reporter where the story is, where the story breaks. The same thing is true if you're on a police beat and have to see the murdered body or the burned bodies being brought out of the fiery building. It's all the same. You live it. And I think it's one of the reasons why news people, as a group, are inclined to be more liberal than others. They live with the common people. I'm talking about the beat reporters. This isn't true of anchorpeople today or of editors sitting back in the home office. But those who are out there with the people understand a great deal more about what the average man and woman have to live through. I think that, in some ways, the high pay of editors and anchorpeople today is unfortunate, because it has removed them from the actual environment of the working man in America. In my early days as a reporter, our salaries were equivalent to a fireman's, a policeman's, a stock clerk's and those were the people we drank with in the evening. Those were the people whose budget problems we understood.

I think there's a great responsibility on the part of war correspondents—to get the story right but not to overdramatize it, which is very difficult to do; to have some appreciation of the military situation that both the G.I.s and the officers themselves are undergoing, not to try to go around them when military necessity dictates

what seem to be onerous restrictions. The war corresponden
very deep responsibility to his country, but no more respo.....
than a reporter in civilian life has—to get it right and be fair and
just.

In the future, I would hope that democracies will understand
that the people have to know what their young people are doing in
their name. When we got to Germany after the war, these rosy-
cheeked German people came to us with tears in their eyes, plead-
ing that they didn't know what was going on under Hitler. That
was their fault. They bore responsibility because they approved the
censorship that Hitler put in, and once they approved that censorship and the people were denied the right to know, they became as
guilty as the perpetrators.


FOR FURTHER READING:
Walter Cronkite, *A Reporter's Life* (Knopf, 1996)

# MARTHA GELLHORN

## SPANISH CIVIL WAR · WORLD WAR II
## VIETNAM

*Martha Gellhorn (1908–1998) became perhaps the best of a particular breed of journalist—the committed partisan who uses the craft on behalf of a cause. She also became addicted to the environment of war, where victims of injustice, cruelty, and folly abound. She wrote about them with a hard-edged compassion that damned their abusers, from Spanish fascists in the 1930s to American strategists in Vietnam.*

*Raised in a progressive and well-to-do St. Louis family in the s1910s and '20s, she was educated at Bryn Mawr, then set out for Europe to become a writer and foreign correspondent. She freelanced for a time in France, where she married and divorced a French peace activist. Returning home during the Great Depression, she investigated strikes for the New Dealer Harry Hopkins and was befriended by*

*Franklin and Eleanor Roosevelt. Like other idealistic young Americans of the 1930s, she felt drawn to the Spanish Civil War and found an ideological home among leftist Republicans fighting a doomed struggle against Francisco Franco's fascists. Another writer in Spain was the novelist Ernest Hemingway. Their five-year marriage saddled Gellhorn with a label she detested but could not escape—"Hemingway's third wife."*

*She covered World War II for* Collier's *in Finland, China, France, Holland, and Germany. Lacking proper press credentials, she smuggled herself across the English Channel in a hospital ship on the day after D Day. She described Nazi torture chambers in liberated Paris. She was at the Elbe River when U.S. and Soviet armies linked against the Germans. She entered the Nazi death camp at Dachau with the first U.S. troops there.*

*After a nine-year marriage to Time-Life editor T. S. Matthews, and long stints living in Mexico and Africa, she reentered the life of a war correspondent in the 1960s, traveling to Israel and Vietnam. By then she was regarded as a relic of another era. Yet her articles about civilian casualties in Vietnam—freelanced to Britain's* Manchester Guardian *because no U.S. publication would back her—are now regarded as classics of war correspondence. Her war reporting was collected in seven books, the best known of which are* The View from the Ground *and* The Face of War. *She also published five novels.*

*For the last twenty years of her life Gellhorn lived mostly in London and in a small cottage in Wales. Her circle of friends included Bill Buford, editor of the literary magazine* Granta, *later fiction editor of the* New Yorker, *and Victoria Glendinning, a British journalist who became a confidante of Gellhorn's after reviewing the writer's book* The Weather in Africa *in the late 1970s. Gellhorn died in 1998.*

———

BILL BUFORD: Martha Gellhorn was a legacy from another time. She was like no one else you've ever met in your life. She was some

character who walked out of a black-and-white movie with a cigarette dangling off the corner of her lip and a glass of whiskey in her
hand. She was Lauren Bacall, but smarter and sexier, and a person
overwhelmingly motivated by questions of justice. There were lots
of sides to Martha. She was a dame; she was a flirt; and she was a
great reporter. That's not a combination that you see very much
now.

VICTORIA GLENDINNING: I think Martha was a rebel. In a way, she
was doing exactly what her family always had done, but in a much
more dramatic way. Her mother had been a great figure in the votes-
for-women movement in St. Louis. Her father was a doctor; there
were a lot of medical men in her family, so there was a tradition of
public service. She never rebelled against her family. She never said,
"I have to get away," or anything like that—though she did get
away and stayed away rather firmly, to make her own life—but it
was the family streak, if you like, coming out in this extraordinary
way, that a woman of an earlier generation wouldn't have been able
to have fulfilled. And indeed, a woman of her generation had to be
pretty feisty in order to do it. In her generation there were not
many women war correspondents. Now, if you look at the television
and the newspapers, there are actually more women war reporters
than there are men, or at least as many. She was not unique, but
she was among a very small band in those days.

For her whole generation, [the Spanish Civil War] was "the
cause." From all over Europe, young poets and writers went off to
fight in Spain, because they realized that it could lead on to something worse, that the fascist threat was real. So for Martha to have
not been involved in Spain would have been unthinkable. She would
have gone there like a magnet to a magnet. It was where the trouble
was. Also, the fact that a Catholic dictator [Francisco Franco] was
making the trouble would be the kind of thing she would have to
see. She was very left-wing, in a certain sense. She would always

take the leftist cause in any conflict—though as a person, she wasn't particularly left-wing, because she had such definite ideas about the ways people should behave and how life should be conducted. She wasn't bohemian in most people's sense of bohemian.

The point about the war in Spain is there was a "for" and there was an "against." It was a very definite conflict; there was no saying "Let's have some reconciliation here." It was about left and right, right and wrong, life and death, and that was really a template for Martha's mentality. I don't think she would have been terribly interested in the modern idea of conflict resolution. She would have just said, "Stop these bastards." But who the bastards are as the world changes and Martha isn't here to tell me is not absolutely clear.

BILL BUFORD: Spain was the great romantic war of the century because it was so simply demarcated between good guys and bad guys. There were those who were defending the Republic; they were looking out for the little guy, and they had a very appealing socialism. Then you had Franco and the fascists. You couldn't have scripted a better war than Spain for shaping the career that Martha Gellhorn would end up having.

———

*Gellhorn began to write articles about the war, particularly about the daily lives of noncombatants in Madrid, for* Collier's. *She spent most of her time in Spain in the company of Ernest Hemingway, whom she had met in Key West—at the bar he made famous, Sloppy Joe's—in 1936. Their relationship was competitive and soon deeply unhappy. They were married on November 21, 1940. Five years later, Hemingway sued for divorce, saying Gellhorn preferred her career to him.*

———

BILL BUFORD: In any dealings with Martha, there was always an essential contract that you would never mention Hemingway. If you

were publishing her book, you couldn't mention him in the b
You couldn't mention him in the biography. You could never r
tion him in the publicity. You could never mention him in any of
the press releases. The first time I mentioned Hemingway to her, it
was one of those drunken evenings [in London late in Gellhorn's
life], and I said, "So... this Hemingway guy..." She said, "William,
when people mention that man's name, I do only one thing. I show
them the door." She didn't show me the door. I had broken the ice.
For the rest of the evening she talked exclusively about Hemingway.

But as much as she didn't want to believe that the man was that
important in her life, he was clearly on some level the most important figure in her life—not just the most important man in her
life, the most important figure. I think she thought he was corrupt.
I think she thought he was lazy. I think she thought he was a boozer.
I think she thought he had no political conscience—an opportunist.
But he had a passion about his sentences which infected her wholly,
and the way she talked about his sentences was often the way she
talked about her sentences.

You would hear Martha talking about sentences that shouldn't
have adjectives. She would be irritated if you stuck in a comma. She
would use conjunctions in a way that made for a rhythm in a sentence. She was talking about a spareness of prose, a kind of staccato
rhythm that you get in Hemingway. To a certain extent you get it
because they're both of the same period. She met Hemingway when
she was just learning the craft herself, when she had notions of what
it was to be a writer, and she found those notions fulfilled and
realized by him. He taught her writing. There's something quite
magical about hearing the lessons of writing from Martha—knowing
these were lessons that she's almost taken verbatim from the Man.

VICTORIA GLENDINNING: If you read her earlier war reporting, it's
very like the work of Hemingway—you know, these short, declar-
ative sentences, and very few adjectives. I sometimes wonder which

came first, the chicken or the egg. I mean, Hemingway's style is so very famous and so very recognizable and so very much his, but I sometimes wonder who learned from whom. Maybe the Hemingway style was really the Martha Gellhorn style. I wouldn't be surprised.

To [her friends], she would say, "Look, it was a terrible mistake. I can say nothing good about that man, so I don't want to talk about him at all." I think it also irritated her to hell that she was Martha Gellhorn, and yet all any interviewer ever really said was, "Hemingway?" She found that outrageous.

I think she found being with one man really boring. She found men on the whole lovely to be with. She wasn't anti-man at all. In fact, most of her close friends were men. She liked dashing young men who did the sort of things that she had done when she was younger. She liked them very much, indeed. But she didn't see the point of having one around all the time.

———

*Gellhorn's disillusionment with Hemingway began early in their relationship. Ward Just, a correspondent for the* Washington Post *when he met Gellhorn in Vietnam, recalled her telling of the time before Pearl Harbor when she and Hemingway learned that Soviet forces had attacked Finland, a key event in the broadening of World War II.*

———

WARD JUST: They're in Idaho. She, Hemingway, Gary Cooper, the movie actor, his wife, and Averell Harriman [heir to a railroad fortune, later the Democratic governor of New York] are shooting ducks. They're listening to the radio one night and the Soviets have invaded Finland. So Martha looks at her wristwatch and says, "Well, Hem, let's go! Let's get the train and get out of here and get to New York and get over to the front!" Hemingway wants no part of it. He's perfectly happy there in the chalet with Averell Harriman, Gary Cooper, Mrs. Cooper, and all the ducks.

So Gellhorn says, "Well, all right, if you're not going to go with me, I'm certainly not sitting here. I'm going alone."

So with that, she gets on the train, gets to New York, smuggles herself aboard a freighter, and locks herself in the john and doesn't emerge until twelve hours later, when the freighter is too far out to turn around and send her back. She was tremendously bold. When she wanted to do something, there was nothing on God's green earth that was going to stand in her way. She gets to Finland, she covers the war, she comes back through Europe, and eventually gets back to the United States a year later.

She said, "Can you imagine? The war beginning in Europe and Hemingway wouldn't leave because he wanted to shoot more ducks?"

———

*Gellhorn spent most of the war in one combat zone or another, but never as a daily correspondent. Her freedom from daily deadlines allowed her to study the effects of war on soldiers and civilians.*

———

VICTORIA GLENDINNING: She wasn't remotely interested in briefings from generals or handouts from governments or press kits. She had a complete contempt for authority's line and the official line. She never even considered it for a minute. I don't think she even knew it or read it. If somebody said, "No, you can't go over that route," or, "No, you can't go there," she took no notice at all. She was going to go there. She mistrusted governments and people of authority profoundly. The collected book of her war reporting is called *The View from the Ground*. She wanted to be on the ground, where the people were who were suffering the brunt of war, to see what really was going on. A lot of her reporting was about the streets of the bombed cities, the women and the children, above all, the children. Being a woman and writing often about the suffer-

ings of women and children, she could have done the kind of
tenderhearted-agony kind of writing. But it was always hard, hard,
tight as a knot, quite stern, austere writing, which made the awful
things she was describing much more so. She was a remarkable,
remarkable writer. The core of Martha really was: There's something terrible going on; who are the baddies? Who are the goodies?
She was very firm about that.

She was certainly a fierce person, and I think a very moral person, in a rather stern way. I mean, there are some kinds of moralities
that will see the other side of the case and say, "Your morality is
for you, my morality is for me." None of that. *She* was moral and
she thought the world was terrible and wicked. She admired strong
morality in other people very much. She admired Eleanor Roosevelt
very, very much; she called Eleanor "the moral true north."

I think Martha thought reporting wars was—she used these
words—"the honorable course." You had to do something, and the
only thing she could do was tell it how it was. She didn't think of
it as particularly glamorous, though she was like an old warhorse,
really—the mere smell of a war and she was off, right into her
eighties. I think she found peace much more difficult. She once
wrote or said, "Reporting wars is what I do." That's what she
thought she was made for.

She talked about the discomfort and the boredom [of war re-
porting]. If you were going to be there at the right moment and
write the piece that is exhilarating to write and to read, you sometimes had to put up with weeks of hanging around, not finding the
right people, being prepared to hang in there, getting sick, waiting
for the right moment and the right time. There's a lot of endurance
involved.

She was a very pretty woman and she could often get onto military planes or through barricades by using that. She never talked
about that side of things, and I remember once asking her, "You

were very pretty, Martha—do you think that helped with your career?" And she looked at me through a cloud of cigarette smoke—she was now eighty-something—and said, "It didn't hurt."

BILL BUFORD: Martha was motivated by questions of justice and injustice. Injustice filled her with rage. Racism filled her with rage. Persecution of the poor filled her with rage. The subjects that have interested her have consistently been instances of injustice—the Jews in the camps, the Nazis in World War II, the United States in Vietnam. These things have driven her out into the field to bear witness. As a reporter, what she always wanted to do was bear witness to some act of injustice so that the world knew. Because if she didn't, or someone else didn't, the world wouldn't know. She had a duty and a responsibility as a journalist to be there, to tell people what she'd seen. Some of her best journalism was just that—just being there and seeing something. She was also driven by a determination to observe details—what people were wearing, what they had to eat, what they were suffering. So much of Martha's writing is just detail. It's just being there, bearing witness, getting the description, knowing that she's in a privileged spot. She's seeing something that we can't see, don't know about, and her job is to make us interested in it and to know of it.

Martha was a person very comfortable in her prejudices. She never felt she had to defend them. She entered World War II seeing it in a very Gellhorn dichotomy of good and evil, and Germany was evil. When she went to Germany, she just recoiled. I think that for her, this was not a Hitler evil; it was some kind of cultural character that produced this evil. She loathed Germany. At one point [after World War II], when the Germans got interested in publishing her, a deal fell through. I remember her writing the letter saying, "Thank God. The last thing I want to do is appear in German." She was full of so much loathing of Germans that I can

*:* publishing some things by her that astonished my German
can remember some things we published by her in England
ally resulted in German television crews coming over to the
office to record images of the publishing house that was publishing
this hate literature about Germany. The hate literature, of course, was
Martha Gellhorn's.

I think she was burned out by the experience of being one of
the first journalists to step into the concentration camps, and the
horror of that experience lived with her for a long time. I think it
went deep and became very, very personal. It's very hard for any
writer of any sensibility to experience that kind of thing.

———

*After covering the Nazi war crimes trials at Nuremberg, Gellhorn wrote*
*relatively little journalism for twenty years. She adopted a son and*
*lived for several years in Mexico, then in Italy. She worked on novels*
*and wrote magazine pieces only occasionally. She married T. S. Mat-*
*thews in 1954 and attempted to lead a settled life in England, but only*
*for a time. She was, as she said of one of her fictional characters, "a*
*traveler in life."*

———

BILL BUFORD: After Hemingway and World War II, she went into
a kind of slumber, and I don't quite understand it. She was married
to Tom Matthews, a man she thought never really loved her. During
that time, I think she tried to do something that she was really not
accustomed to doing and should never have tried. I think she tried
to be a good wife. I don't think anybody should try to be a good
wife in any time, but Martha, of all people—there was no way in
the world she could have been a good wife. And Vietnam was the
thing that sort of shook her out of her slumber. Vietnam, I think,
woke her up as a writer.

———

*Gellhorn had declared she would not cover a war again. But in the early 1960s she was on the move again—Poland, Israel, Africa. She and Matthews divorced in 1963. She was an early opponent of the U.S. effort to shore up a non-Communist regime in South Vietnam, and when the American presence expanded in 1965, she decided to write about it. On the basis of two months in Vietnam—August and September 1966—she covered dark elements of the U.S. war effort that her colleagues in the mainstream press would not write about widely until several more years had passed.*

*As the basis of her investigation, she chose a sentence from an official lecture given to U.S. soldiers: "To really and truly and finally win this war we must… win the hearts and minds of the people of South Vietnam." She soon concluded that U.S. forces were unintention-ally killing several times as many South Vietnamese civilians as the Vietcong guerrillas were. "This is indeed a new kind of war, as the indoctrination lecture stated," she wrote, "and we had better find a new way to fight it. Hearts and minds, after all, live in bodies."*

———

BILL BUFORD: I know she had trouble finding a paper that would take her on. She ended up stringing for the *Guardian* [of Manchester, England]. I think she went over on her own nickel, and the only thing the *Guardian* really offered was a venue. The *Guardian* is this great, liberal ragbag of a paper, and [the editors] may or may not have known who Martha Gellhorn was. It would have been liberal and anti-American and very indulgent of these extreme, highly par-tisan views of this genius war reporter.

WARD JUST: You have to understand how she looked. When I knew her, she was in her mid-fifties. She was a wonderful-looking woman, and she had this voice. It was a whiskey voice. It was sort of low and it was kind of melodious, and she had an almost permanently cocked eyebrow. It took very little pushing to get her to talk about life in World War II and life in Spain. She had a wonderful memory for anecdote.

What made her such an attractive character was that she was still an ideologue. In my time [in Vietnam], we were edging up into the postmodern world. She was still back in Spain and World War II, where you had the fascists on one hand and the good guys on the other. That was one reason why she despised the war in Vietnam. She said that of all the wars she had covered—and she'd covered about eighteen by the time she died—Vietnam was the only war she reported from the wrong side.

When I knew her, she was spending a lot of time in civilian hospitals, looking at the results of the misguided bombs and the artillery shells and the care, specifically but not exclusively, of women and children—children who had had their limbs destroyed and sometimes their minds destroyed, also. I knew about her reputation as a pure war correspondent in World War II, and I thought, God, what a waste to spend your time doing that. Then, when I had been in the war zone a little longer myself, I began to see that she had been on to something very, very serious. I mean, we all knew about civilian casualties and paid a certain amount of attention to them, but the mainstream correspondents did not go into it in the kind of detail that Martha did.

Those pieces of hers were wonderfully written, without any sappiness to them. That's the last thing Martha Gellhorn was—a sap. She was a very tough-minded woman. These pieces would go marching down the page, one sentence after another, and at the end of it you realized what a horror we had created. You saw it yourself. You had known it in some abstract way, but for the first time you could see it with precision. That was Martha Gellhorn.

She had a wonderful theory that's certainly true, from my ob-

servation. She thought that all successful military officers had a kind
of gaiety about them. What she meant by that was a sort of deep-
running good cheer—a jauntiness and a kind of truculence that was
so attractive that other men would follow them. That's the way she
saw the best of the American commanders in World War II. In
Vietnam, on the other hand, she went along on a few military actions
and she said, "You know, your officers"—talking to me, as if I com-
manded them; she identified me with them—"your officers have got
their helmets on all the time. There's not an enemy within miles.
Why do you suppose that is, Ward? Do you think it could be because they know they're losing?" You scratched your head and figured, yeah, maybe she's got something there.

VICTORIA GLENDINNING: You could imagine that somebody like
Martha Gellhorn would be a terrific feminist, and, in fact, there have
been attempts to make her a kind of icon of feminism. But she wasn't
interested in that, because she couldn't see the point. She said:
"Why, if you're a woman, does it make a difference? Why doesn't
everybody, man or woman or beast, just get on with it and do what
they want to do?" And I would say things like, "Well, Martha, it's
very difficult for some women; they feel they won't be able to do
that." She said, "Well, why ever not? Just go and do it like I did."

     She was republished by a very fine feminist publishing house
here [in England]. They brought all her fiction back into print, in
fact, which was a wonderful thing to do, and she was very pleased
about it. But she wasn't pleased about being classed as a feminist
writer. It wasn't the point, at all. She was a writer. She was writing
for anybody who would read it.

BILL BUFORD: Martha was always amused at how she'd been taken
up by the feminists. They would write her letters; they would say
they wanted to write books about her; and every now and then she'd
go out to lunch with them and come away perplexed. She had a

combination—which is more politically acceptable now than it would have been ten or twenty years ago—of being a fighter, looking out for herself, and of being a complete babe. She was the most flirtatious woman I've ever known.

She was different with women. She was more demanding. She was often more intellectual. She was more critical. She was fine with women. But she flourished in the company of men. Her evenings in London were often organized around the visits of men. She had lots of young men friends. I remember at her wake, after her death, we all gathered, all her friends, and there were a handful of women, quite a lot of them bruised by Martha, although in truth, all of us at one time or another got bruised by Martha. But there were mainly a lot of men. She adored men.

I'm pretty sure the first time I met her was long after we'd been corresponding and long after I'd been privileged enough to have published some of her writing in the literary magazine I was editing then, called *Granta*. The most astonishing thing about Martha then was simply the realization that she was still alive. This was a woman well into her eighties who was, after all, Hemingway's third wife; who had covered every modern confrontation in the twentieth century; and here she was living in England, where I was. Someone had suggested that I approach her for a special issue on travel writing. I did. We celebrated it with a party at the poet James Fenton's house in Oxford, and I can remember everybody at that party whispering, "Is that Martha Gellhorn? I didn't know she was alive." She had such an aura about her. She had lived so much of the twentieth century and she somehow carried the twentieth century with her. There was something very exciting about being in her presence, and what was great about that particular occasion was that a whole room was picking that up. It wasn't just a one-on-one thing. It was a whole room—a sort of buzz going around the room: "That's Martha Gellhorn."

In her eighties she became a kind of cult figure in literary London. She would gather all these writers around her. She'd line one up at six, one at seven, one at eight; then she'd line up another one to go out for dinner. I mean, it was astonishing. This was a woman eighty-five years old who could drink anybody under the table, meanwhile smoking three packs of cigarettes. I don't even know if you could say she was a force of nature. There was something almost profoundly unnatural about her. But she was a profound force.

She needed to experience things alone because then she experienced things more intensely, and she needed to be alone to write. Her life was bifurcated in a very orchestrated fashion between times when she was alone, experiencing whatever it was—you know, swimming naked in her eighties in the Indian Ocean off the Tanzanian coast, where she had someone's house for three months; or sitting on top of this hill in Wales where she would be writing. Then she'd have periods when she needed intense social interactions.

VICTORIA GLENDINNING: I don't think she could have endured the kind of war reporting that people have been forced to do in, say, Afghanistan, where you can't get into the country; you can't get near it; it's all done on spin and handouts. I think the real core of her morality was the cruelty and injustice of war, how it always hits the wrong people. The bigwigs and the politicians and the generals are comfortably out of danger and the small people and the poor people and the civilians—you know, "collateral damage"—are the ones that take the brunt.

BILL BUFORD: When I was editing *Granta,* the articles she continually wanted to do were the ones in which she was enraged about something. She was apoplectic about the fact that the United States decided to take over Panama, and she went down there and bearded some general and said: "What the hell are you doing down here? Just how do you justify this occupation? Just what do you think you're doing?" The basic Martha Gellhorn engine was that some-body had done something wrong and she was going to make sure the world knew about it. Rage motivated her.

Martha believed in a very small number of essential principles. Truth. Honesty. She believed that the underprivileged always got a raw deal. She believed that people with power can't be trusted. She believed that people with money can't be trusted. But she wasn't really a political thinker. And whenever she had to analyze some-thing—like what was going on in Vietnam, some paragraph artic-ulating why that thing was wrong and how it could be better—she might struggle with that paragraph for weeks. That wasn't her strength. Her strength was in having this basic code, a kind of Robin Hood code. Truth is a good thing; lying is a bad thing. There are good people; there are bad people.

War correspondents are some of the sickest people you'll ever meet. I've been lucky enough to publish quite a few of them—lucky to be in a position where they're going and I'm doing the publishing. There's something wrong with somebody who wants to go where people are being shot. You know, you don't cross the street if traffic's coming at you. If someone's slamming a door in your face, you get out of the way. War correspondents do everything that we don't do. If there's a fight, they try to get close to it. Someone's shooting a gun: "Oh, good, let's go run up to the gun." They are amazing animals. War breaks out and they want to be there. War breaks out and they get really uncomfortable being home.

I think most war correspondents find war fun. You know, there is nothing more exciting than violence. You are in the complete present tense. Every choice counts. Every moment counts. Every second counts. We don't live life that intensely. A war correspondent does.

Having said that, I don't think Martha would ever admit to wars being fun. It wasn't so much that she found war fun as that she

found it comfortable, and she was comfortable when she w
It was her vernacular.

I think journalists cover wars for all kinds of reaso
they're there as a kind of regulating eye about what governments
could get up to. But I don't think war reporters become war reporters because they have this chance to reprimand governments.
That's not why they go there. At its heart, a war is humanity at its
most extreme.

The ones who are really weird, the real screwballs, are the ones
who can still do it, who keep going back for it and can't stop. In a
way, that was what was so compelling about Martha Gellhorn. She
was desperately trying to get a paper to send her to the Gulf War.
She must have been eighty-six. Loopy.

FOR FURTHER READING:

Martha Gellhorn, *The Face of War* (Simon and Schuster, 1959)

————, *The View from the Ground* (Granta Books, 1989)

Carl E. Rollyson, *Nothing Ever Happens to the Brave: The Story of Martha Gellhorn* (St. Martin's Press, 1990)

# ANDY ROONEY

## WORLD WAR II

*On July 7, 1941, five months to the day before the attack on Pearl Harbor, Andy Rooney submitted to the Selective Service and entered the U.S. Army. By his own admission he was not prime warrior material. He had grown up in a comfortably well-off family in Albany, New York, and attended a fine prep school, the Albany Academy. At the academy he took part in a student drill team "in which I learned to detest everything military at an early age," he wrote in* My War, *his memoir. While he was a college student at Colgate, World War II began in Europe, and the Roosevelt administration made moves toward intervening. Rooney was against it. "I didn't want to go to Europe to fight and die for what seemed to me to be someone else's cause." He considered applying for exemption from the draft as a conscientious*

*objector. But after "many long, sophomoric discussions with my friends,"
he concluded that "while I was an objector, I could not honestly claim
to be a conscientious one." So he reported for duty.*

*He was assigned to the Seventeenth Field Artillery Regiment,
where he spent much of his time as the clerk for the regimental band.
"The prospects of being killed at war," he recalled, "seemed remote."
But the editors of the* Stars and Stripes, *the official daily newspaper
of the Army, accepted Rooney's application for a transfer. His prospects
for seeing action increased dramatically, and the path of his career
was set.*

*The* Stars and Stripes *was a major newspaper with a large staff
that included editors and reporters already prominent or soon to become
so. The paper published editions all over the world and sent correspondents to cover every campaign. Rooney, though one of the staff's
youngest reporters, became one of its best, getting assignments that included the invasion of Normandy and the drive across France and
Germany to Berlin. He walked through the extermination camp at
Buchenwald just after its liberation, and worked alongside such reporters as Ernie Pyle and Homer Bigart. Rooney's recollection of Pyle
is especially interesting, since Rooney's own postwar writings have carried a plainspoken eloquence rather like the style that made readers feel
so affectionate toward Pyle.*

*After the war, Rooney became a freelance writer, then a newspaper
columnist, and in the 1970s he became one of the most recognized figures
in broadcasting as the regular commentator on CBS News's 60*
Minutes. *His memoirs and collections of commentary have been best-
sellers.*

*In 1942 and 1943 Rooney lived in London while writing about
the air war. It was a safe assignment until he and several other
correspondents applied to go along on a mission, the same one that took
Walter Cronkite and Homer Bigart on a raid over Wilhelmshaven,
Germany.*

———

We were covering the air war in England—eight or ten reporters writing about the Eighth Air Force. I met Walter Cronkite in London, and we traveled a lot together. Another great friend was Gladwin Hill, who was with the Associated Press, later with the *New York Times.* And there was a man named Bob Post, who was the *New York Times* reporter.

Every time there was a raid, we would split up and each go to a different bomber group. Then, when the crews came back, we would interview them. And sometimes they didn't come back. We, on the other hand, went back to our flats in London and lived quite a comfortable life. After a while, we saw so many people we had gotten to know who were shot down, taken prisoner, or killed that we all began to feel guilty about covering this war the way we were. It just seemed wrong to us. I don't know who decided to do it, but we decided we'd better go on a bombing raid ourselves. Though correspondents were never supposed to man a gun or carry any kind of a weapon, we were all forced to go to a gunnery school; we practiced gunnery in case they needed us in the air.

[On each raid] they were losing 5 to 6 percent of all the bombers that went out. There were twenty-five bombers, give or take one or two, in each bomber group, and each crew had to do twenty-five missions. Well, if you have to do twenty-five missions in a group of twenty-five planes, and you're losing 5 percent, it doesn't take any mathematical genius to know their chances of finishing were not good, and not many finished twenty-five missions. I think maybe 15 or 20 percent finished twenty-five missions successfully and were allowed to go home.

The raid we went on was only the second raid into Germany. It was on Wilhelmshaven. I got in my bomber and I thought to myself, "Why am I doing this? I'm scared to death. I mean, I don't have to risk my life"—except that I felt so bad for all the men who did have to risk their lives all those times that it just seemed like it was the honest thing to do. I remember we had these heavy flak jackets. A B-17 is not like a modern airliner. Wires and everything were all over, and getting through the bomb bay to the back—which would be the cabin in a passenger plane now—was very difficult. If you had a parachute on, it was tough to get past all the wires without getting snagged on everything. So I didn't wear my flak jacket. I stood on it. I had this feeling that I didn't want to be hit from underneath, but of course what happened was the flak exploded in the air around you and didn't necessarily come from below.

If there was flak before you got to the target, the pilot could take evasive action. But once the bombsight zeroed in on the target, you couldn't take any evasive action or the bombs would not go where they were designed to go. That plane was a perfect target for the gunners from underneath, and that was the frightening part of it—you just had to sit there.

There were seven of us [reporters] who actually went, and I was the youngest, but I ended up with the best story because my bomber was hit. I was up in the nose of the plane, and a shell came and took a small piece of the Plexiglas nose off. The bombardier, who was in front of me, panicked and tried to stuff something in the hole. At seventeen or eighteen thousand feet, that air coming in is subzero, and he took his gloves off. His hands froze and it was terrible. I looked across at the little desk that the navigator used. His oxygen tube had been pierced and he lost his oxygen, and at eighteen thousand feet he collapsed. So I got to the pilot intercom and I asked him what to do. He said, "Well, we have emergency air in oxygen bottles up behind me. Take some deep breaths and come back up behind me and get the oxygen bottle; bring it back down and hook him up to that." Well, I didn't know how to do any of this and here I was, with somebody's life at stake, and I didn't know how long you lasted once you took your oxygen mask off. But I took some deep breaths, I took my oxygen mask off, and went through this alleyway up behind the pilot. There I got an oxygen bottle and hooked up the navigator, who was a much more experienced flyer than the bombardier. He regained consciousness and got the bombardier quieted down. So I had by far the best story to tell of all the correspondents who went out that day.

I'm always embarrassed to read something I've written years ago. I look at things I wrote in high school and college and they always seem so bad. I'll write a column today and I'll read it a week from today and think, "Gosh, I could do better than that; I hope I'm better than that now." Anyway, I'm a little embarrassed to read this, but this was my lead about the trip to Wilhelmshaven:

"U.S. bomber station, February 26th. From the nose of Lieutenant Bill Casey's bomber, I saw American Fortresses and Liberators drop a load of destruction on Wilhelmshaven today. We flew to Germany in the last group of a Fortress formation, and my ship, the *Banshee,* was in the trailing squadron. Soon after dawn the bombers thundered down the runway. Lieutenant Casey's windshield was splattered with mud on the way; it really was a blind take-off. Like a pick-up football team on a Saturday morning we grew in strength as we flew until all England seemed to be covered with bombers. Everything was quiet, almost monotonous, for an hour after we left the English coast. Then the trouble began.... Out of the sun came shining silver German fighting planes diving at one bomber in the formation and disappearing below the cloud banks as quickly as they had come. They seemed tiny, hardly a machine of destruction, and an impossible target for our gunners..."

———

*More than five hundred reporters, photographers, and cameramen were accredited to Supreme Headquarters, Allied Expeditionary Force (SHAEF) to cover the cross-Channel invasion of France in 1944. But*

*only twenty-eight specially trained "assault correspondents" were as-*
*signed to accompany the first waves of troops that went ashore on D*
*Day, June 6, 1944—and a blunder by the Army left nine of those*
*twenty-eight stranded in England for several days.*

———

There was no way for a reporter to cover D Day unless he was
there, and I was not there, and very few reporters were there. I've
always been irritated by people who claim to have been there on
D Day but were not. I came in on D-plus-four, which was not a
safe time to come in either. By that time the graves registration unit
had been able to collect a lot of the bodies and they had them laid
out on the beaches. They put blankets over their faces, and I
thought, all these young boys, all so different and their shoes all the
same. I remember that hit me, and it was one of the few vivid
memories I have that I have never lost—the scene of the dead on
the beach, lying there.

Every soldier who went ashore knew what happened within just
a few yards of him. He knew too much about it. He saw a friend
shot through the head, shot through the stomach, drown in shallow
water. But he had no idea what was really happening. I remember
being irritated when I read what they were issuing from SHAEF in
London. They said what a success the invasion had been. They
didn't see anybody killed. And of course they were right and those
of us who saw what had happened on the beaches were wrong. It
*had* been a success. It didn't look like a success if you saw the boys
getting killed.

———

*In the early weeks in Normandy, as the Allied armies tried to consol-*
*idate their gains and build up forces for a "breakout" across France,*
*infantry units fought across farm fields bordered by hedgerows—dense*

*thickets of foliage and earth that provided perfect cover for the fiercely resisting Germans.*

———

"Move out"—that was the dreaded phrase. "Movin' out, movin' out." They would whisper it from one man to the next, and he would turn and say, "Movin' out, movin' out." You dreaded to hear it because you knew you were going to have to go over that hedgerow and take the next hedgerow, perhaps with Germans behind it.

We were all just reporters, and we would get to a certain point behind the lines [and stop]—not safe, but still, we didn't have to climb over that hedgerow and go across the open field under machine gun fire. So there was a certain feeling of guilt that I think most reporters had.

There were about twenty-five correspondents covering the First Army, which was the major army going across Europe. We would all get up in the morning, twenty-five correspondents, with about sixteen or eighteen jeeps. Ernie Pyle would sit there in his tent and be indecisive about where he would go that day. Very often he would not go up to the front. Here we were, trying to get the hot story, and Ernie would go back to the Tenth Shoe Repair Battalion or something like that and get a better story than all the rest of us at the front.

Pyle was very close to the image the American public had of him. He was slight, for one thing. He was a small man with gray hair and he always wore that little wool cap, olive drab—a helmet liner, actually. I was in my tent one day and Ernie was lying on a cot just opposite from me. I hadn't gone out that day; I was trying to make some notes. Right below me there was a hole in the ground, and some bees started going down into it. Ernie was reading. I finally got up and scuffed dirt over the hole. Other bees came and they couldn't find the hole—all their friends were down there. So we watched a while and we obviously had the same thought, and finally Ernie looked at me and he says, "Aw, Andy, let 'em out." He even felt sorry for the bees I had trapped down there. That was the kind of guy Ernie Pyle was.

I suppose there was a certain amount of imitation [of Pyle] because we all heard how popular his work was. He was not doing so much war reporting as feature stories about people *in* the war. It was very attractive to people back home, finding out what they were like.

There was very little offensive censorship. As correspondents, we all knew which side we were on, which was not necessarily true in Vietnam, where there was so much vacillation about who was right and who was wrong. But we were all Americans and we all wanted our side to win the war, so we did not want to do anything that could possibly damage our side. We knew what the rules were. We had two censors traveling with us in the First Army press camp at all times. They read everything we wrote but very seldom took anything out, because we knew what we could write and what we couldn't write. We did not reveal any positions or troop concentrations or numbers of troops or anything like that. There was no censorship that we found objectionable.

I [once] saw something that I didn't try to write. I was in Normandy. Our troops were moving forward quickly and we were overrunning German positions. We were running over German troops faster than we could take prisoners, and an army moving forward can't spare any soldiers to guard prisoners. We came to this French farmhouse and there was this door that went down into the cellar, and it was open, and there were five Germans lying there in pools of blood with a white flag on a pole. They had come up out of the basement to surrender and had been machine-gunned down by American soldiers.

I was shocked, and I don't think the American public would

understand that. They do not like to think of American
doing that. I understand why it happened. They were afraid
ican soldiers were afraid for their own lives. Here were these five
Germans; they did not have time to take them prisoner; they didn't
want them wandering around. Shot them. Understandable. Wrong,
but understandable in that kind of action. That sort of story might
not have been written.

———

*The Nazi effort to exterminate European Jewry had been reported in
American newspapers from an early point in the war. But the reports
were often discounted as exaggerated; some feared they were a reprise
of the exaggerated claims of German atrocities in World War I. The
full horror of the Nazis' crimes did not break into Americans' consciousness until the liberation of the concentration camps in the spring
of 1945. Correspondents, including Rooney, were among the first to see
the evidence.*

———

When I was in college I thought I was a pacifist. I had a professor
there who was a pacifist, and he had indoctrinated me, and I almost
registered as a conscientious objector. I was drafted and got to the
war and went across Europe. When I got to Buchenwald, I thought,
"Wow, how wrong can one person be?" I had seen a lot up till that
time, but there was nothing like Buchenwald. I was just embarrassed
for how wrong I had been, thinking we had no business in that war.
I thought to myself that I would like to take that professor by the
hand and lead him through what I was seeing here at Buchenwald—
see if he's still a pacifist.

We had such great access to the action [in World War II]—which
reporters of current wars have not had—that we provided much
greater service to the American public. Our military brass allowed

us to cover the war. The Pentagon has not allowed that in the last few conflicts we have been in, so that much of what has happened in war has been hidden from the American public. It's dishonest, it's wrong, and it does not allow a democracy to do what it should do, and that's to decide what actions we should take. If you don't know the facts, you can't vote intelligently.

I fail to understand why the American public accepted the clamps that the Pentagon put on the media [in the 1980s and '90s]. I mean, in a democracy, it is unacceptable. Occasionally, a reporter will do something that damages an army's [safety], but very seldom. I mean, it is so much more likely that damage will be done by a lack of information than by giving too much information in a story. Almost always, the enemy knows what it is the Pentagon is trying to keep from the American public.

In World War II, it was very difficult to show the American public what was happening because the cameramen—the motion-picture photographers—were carrying 35-millimeter cameras that weighed 170 pounds, and they could not go up to the front to show anybody what was happening. Now, you have a camera that you can put in your pocket, and it is much easier to show people what is really happening—except that most reporters and photographers have been prevented from going where the action is to show the American public.

A reporter should be sitting over at the side watching what's happening. He should not be part of what is happening.

Almost always, the best way to write a story is just to put one little word down after the other until you have it. A reporter should basically present the facts, and if in the course of that he turns a nice phrase, well, that may be additional, but great writing doesn't have much of a place in reporting. That would be a controversial statement with a lot of reporters, but that's my feeling.

I think journalism is a rough draft of history. Reporters are not conscious of it because they are covering [only] this one little bit of the story that they see. But if they report what's happening from day to day, it is part of the great panorama of history.

FOR FURTHER READING:

Andrew A. Rooney, *My War* (Times Books, 1995)

FCCJ ARCHIVES

# FRANK GIBNEY

## KOREA

*Frank Gibney was Time-Life bureau chief in Japan when war broke out in Korea in 1950. At a distance of more than fifty years, he reminds post–Cold War readers of the deep sense of peril that affected Americans in the years immediately after World War II. "All you saw around you was a total montage of aggression," he says. The Soviet Union was consolidating its hold on Eastern Europe and testing atomic weapons. Mao Zedong's Communists were triumphant in China. When Soviet-backed North Koreans attacked South Korea in June 1950, Gibney says, "We really thought the Russians were out to destroy us." That was the context for the reporters who covered the war in Korea—that, and the imperious leadership of General Douglas MacArthur, the shogun of occupied Japan, who returned to command United Nations forces (most of them American) in Korea.*

*In World War II, Gibney had served as a U.S. Naval Intelligence officer in the Pacific theater, where he interrogated Japanese prisoners of war. After Korea he worked for* Newsweek *and* Life, *then left journalism for a varied career as an educator, speechwriter (for President Lyndon Johnson), policy consultant, editor, and author. A leading authority on East Asian and Asia-Pacific affairs, he became a professor of politics at Pomona College in California and president of the Pomona-based Pacific Basin Institute.*

———

We first heard about the Korean War on a memorable Sunday morning at the press club in Tokyo. Many of the correspondents used to gather there for breakfast or brunch. Everyone was somewhat shocked. I had just come back from Korea, where I had been on an extensive reporting tour a month before, and I must confess that I hadn't thought the war would happen this soon. But it happened. The first thing everyone did, of course, was to get out of there and back to the public information office of MacArthur's SCAP [Supreme Command, Allied Powers] and find out how we could get over there. There's a war, so you have to cover it.

I'll always remember Ernie Hoberecht, who was then the bureau chief of United Press, having a few drafts of his coffee and then turning around and saying reflectively, "Well, time to get back to the office and start grinding out the atrocity stories." He was all too correct. That was a self-fulfilling prophecy.

———

*By the early afternoon of June 26, 1950, the public information office at MacArthur's headquarters in Japan was thronged with reporters trying to wangle their way onto an outbound military flight to Korea. Typically, the advantage went to the news outlets with the largest circulations. Gibney and three other Americans—Burton Crane of the*

*New York Times, Marguerite Higgins of the New York Herald Tribune, and Keyes Beech of the Chicago Daily News—scored the only available seats on an Air Force C-54 that was scheduled to depart for Seoul the next morning.*

———

We had a lot of baggage with us. Marguerite had a huge suitcase that looked like a trunk and the Air Force said they weren't going to carry that sort of thing over to Korea. So Marguerite, in some desperation, said, "Can you put a few things in one of your packs?" So I said, "Yep, you can fill up my backpack," and so she did.

We landed at Kimpo Airfield [near Seoul, the South Korean capital], and got ready to go into Seoul. There was the most amazing scene in front of us—all these cars from the State Department and related dependents, parked. The owners were all being evacuated— they had left their cars there. So we had our choice of any kind of car we wanted. Some of us took convertibles, a few of us took a jeep, and we drove into Seoul. [Crane, Beech, and I] bedded down at a house of a U.S. Army lieutenant colonel there, who was a friend. We had a few drinks and went to bed. At two or three in the morning, the telephone rang. There was apparently an anguished conversation, then our friend said: "They've broken through. Head south." He climbed into his jeep to go back to KMAG [Korean Military Advisory Group] headquarters, so there was nothing for us to do but to climb into our jeep and try to follow him.

We drove into Seoul, then out. We were on the Han River Bridge, following the traffic that was heading south, pell mell. The troops were going south and we were going with them. We joined the traffic on this vastly overcrowded bridge over the River Han. As we went onto the bridge, there was this tremendous explosion. We thought we were being bombed from the air. We were hit by pieces of flying glass. In front of us there was a huge truckload full of Korean Army MPs on their way south. God help them, they were blown up, because they got the full force of the blast. Crane, Beech, and I got out of the jeep. Crane and I had both been injured. We rushed over to the riverbank and tried to mop up the blood that was streaming from our faces. I reached into my backpack to get some bandages, but all I could find were Marguerite Higgins's pants—a rather jazzy blue and white ensemble. And so I used them to mop up the blood. She was very useful in that regard.

We got down to Suwon just after MacArthur arrived for a quick look. Our trip was embarrassing. As we drove along the road the Koreans would see us—already there were refugees heading south—and they were clapping. I felt ashamed because as Americans we should have been protecting them; we shouldn't be heading south.

We still thought that we had been bombed. We didn't know then that the South Korean Army had blown up the bridge by mistake. The chief of staff had panicked. All of us thought this was the beginning of World War III.

We ended up at Suwon, where the South Korean Army—or what was left of it—was trying to regroup. From there I was evacuated to a U.S. Army hospital in Japan.

———

*Gibney soon began a weekly shuttle schedule, racing back and forth between Korea and his office in Tokyo. Like the war itself, press policy in Korea was improvised on the run. No arrangements were made for correspondents' transportation. At press headquarters in Taejon, there was only one military phone line to Tokyo. Reporters had to take turns shouting their copy for a few rationed minutes between midnight and 4 A.M. For the rest of the day, the line was off limits. "Never since and including the Civil War," Associated Press columnist Hal Boyle groused, "have correspondents had so few of the facilities vital to their trade."*

———

After I had my head bandaged up, I flew back to Korea. Since I was working for *Time* and *Life,* I had so much to report that it was impossible to file through normal channels. So each week I had to jump on the plane back to Tokyo, where I would write first the *Time* file, then the *Life* file, and then do stories for two Japanese magazines and one Japanese newspaper, because at that time Japanese correspondents were not allowed in Korea.

Getting [the story] out is always difficult. My heart goes out to the people who had to go through the minutiae of military censorship. It wasn't bad at first. But gradually, as the staff of the public information officer increased, there were more guys around to censor things.

MacArthur was very sensitive to criticism. He was generally protected by the three wire services. The bureau chiefs of Associated Press, United Press, and International News Service were widely known in the press corps as "the Palace Guard." The Palace Guard was always allowed on MacArthur's aircraft, and they reported faithfully what the general had in mind, and it was often far from the true picture.

There was no [formal system of] censorship of reporting in Korea, but if a correspondent filed something that was at variance with official reports, he would hear about it and maybe his principals in the United States would hear about it, too. It was a kind of never-never land. I never faced that, because I had so much to file that I always flew back to Japan, where there was no interference whatsoever. Yet even within the *Time* and *Life* community, there was great conflict. David Douglas Duncan, the great *Life* photographer, flew in and, with true Marine intolerance, denounced the whole South Korean Army as "a bunch of yardbirds" who were no good. I then wrote an article in *Life* denouncing Duncan's view of the Korean Army. Actually, there were two Korean divisions that fought off the North Koreans at the beginning of the war, and the United States had given them no artillery.

We had another issue in the press corps—whether to carry a gun or not. According to the Geneva Convention, war correspondents were supposed to be unarmed. That was part of their mystique. On the other hand, many of us were nervous about that, because in the Korean War you never knew when you were going to run into a nest of guerrillas, or whether people who were dressed as Korean farmers would turn out to be North Korean troops or irregulars. There were a lot of Communist irregulars in the south. So some of us, myself included, went back to Tokyo, bought weapons and shoulder holsters, and wore them through the war. My view was that I was damned if I was going to be shot without having a chance to shoot the other fellow.

The Korean War was a case of total aggression by the Communist side. Even years later, when I faced this issue with my Chinese friends, they would say, "Well, you know, the South started the Korean War." And I would say, "To hell with that. I was there and I heard the Soviet advisers over the intercom and I know who started it." Whereupon my friends in the Chinese Communist hierarchy would just say "Hee, hee, hee" because they knew, too. So this was a war of total aggression. Many of us were unaware at the time that there were atrocities on the South Korean side, too, because the atrocities the North perpetrated were so flagrant. I mean, they would come into the city of Seoul and find as many leading citizens as they could and shoot them. It was a war where you did not want to be taken prisoner. So, to my mind—and I think to the minds of most correspondents—there was no conflict of interest at all. We were reporting a war for civilization against the forces of evil.

In this day and age, we can sit back and say, "Well, that was the Cold War mystique, and it was all overdrawn." Yet you must put yourself back in that period, where all you saw around you was a total montage of aggression. In Europe, when I was there in '47 and '48, the Soviets took over Czechoslovakia. They'd already taken over Poland, not to mention Hungary. In China you had Mao Zedong, who was getting more anti-American by the minute. We really thought the Russians were out to destroy us. So there was no divergence of opinion there. There was a sense that we were fighting for survival.

———

*Still, the correspondents in Korea tended to be quite open about the military debacles in the field. At one point, in late June 1950, MacArthur tossed seventeen correspondents out of the war zone and accused the correspondents as a group of being traitors. He also extended the voluntary censorship guidelines to forbid any criticism of United Nations commanders or Allied performance in the field. But it wasn't until December 21, 1950—after the Chinese joined North Korea—that formal censorship was finally imposed. After that, the press was much more dependent on the military for information.*

———

The very word "briefing" bothers me. In the Korean War, if someone said, "There is going to be a briefing at MacArthur's headquarters," my first impulse was to ignore it. I'd go and talk to a colonel I knew and ask him what was going on. When you find a screen interposed between you and the news, you want to penetrate the screen, and there are lots of ways to penetrate it. When I was a reporter, I would defy you to give me a situation—other than, say, the problems of reporting something from North Korea or Stalin's Russia—where there was not some way of going around to a fellow who knew what was going on and asking him.

The correspondents who came from far places to cover the war had no experience in dealing with MacArthur's headquarters. Those of us who were based in Tokyo knew all too well the problem of MacArthur and censorship, either imposed or implied. MacArthur's headquarters would try to manage the news in a very offensive way, and the correspondents in Tokyo were prepared to resist this. We separated the official view of MacArthur and Company from what was really happening. And that's why many of us diverged from what City Hall was saying. Even within SCAP headquarters, there were divergences of opinion, and of course there were divergences of opinion within the U.S. Army. I accompanied General Walton "Johnny" Walker on some of his trips to Korea just before he was killed, and he was very vocal about the bad training of the troops, and how he'd been given infantry that literally couldn't fight.

I was prepared to discount what was officially said about Korea at the MacArthur level when I talked to a regimental commander or a divisional commander, especially someone I knew. You always had to make distinctions about who was giving you the information. MacArthur had deployed a vast publicity apparatus, ultimately with the hope of making himself president of the United States. Thank God we escaped that.

The colonels and majors talked to us quite freely, and it was, in a sense, a band of brothers. We were all fighting the same war, and I didn't feel any conflict at all. Only when we got into dealing with what MacArthur's headquarters was saying did I know there was a real conflict between the attempt to impose a point of view and the point of view that we had.

The American press deserves the title of "Fourth Estate," which means that you are not supposed to be part of the establishment. You were supposed to always take one step backward. Now, this does not say that you were supposed to be automatically against the establishment, and, I must say, when I was reporting later in Europe and in Asia, I would make decisions on my own about what to report and what not to report. For example, if there was something that really embarrassed the United States in the role we were playing at that time, I might suppress it or I might not suppress it. But it was my call. That, to me, is the essential difference between having a subservient press and having an independent press. The man on the spot always has to feel it's his call, and that's the way I always reported.

I just saw the beginnings of Vietnam. I went there only once in 1965 and took a look around. I was there for two days when I got a call from some general saying, "Hey, Frank, we've got a good deal coming up. We're going to leave at three in the morning and bust some Vietcong, really rough 'em up. Do you want to come along?" I sat back and reflected—"Saipan, Okinawa, the Korean War, Inchon." And I said, "Gosh, General, I'm afraid I'm about to take the plane to Tokyo."

It seems to me the only thing more interesting than the way the Pentagon was able to make the press seem irrelevant in the [Persian Gulf War] was the degree to which the press pretty much lay down and took it. I mean, all the broadcast networks pretty much accepted the "smart bomb" video stuff and all the sexy pictures they were being fed. You didn't have masses of reporters getting arrested. You didn't have anybody trying to break the pool system.

As an old-fashioned journalist, I'd have to say that I think television is at fault here. Because what are the objectives of a TV reporter and a news reporter? The TV reporter's first objective is to get that photo opportunity and pass it on. If you consider the [desire of] the television press to photograph anything and everything and show everyone's point of view, you could put yourself back in the World War II era, and CNN would say, "We have a great scoop here with the Third Reich's *Führer*, Hitler, and we're going to get his story on the Holocaust. What do you think, Hitler? Was it a good thing to kill all those people?" You know, you can

71

ude too far. In the last analysis, you are not from Mars,
l these strange Earthlings. You are an American cor-
and you're going to report the story based on your cul-
background, what you've learned, and what you've
decided is right and wrong. The news reporter has at least a chance
to step back before he writes, but in television you have to get the
picture first. When getting the picture is your principal objective,
you're apt to follow whatever the local spin doctors tell you as long
as they'll let you get the picture. So I think television reporting has
been very damaging, and I don't think it has found its way to an
ethic yet. Maybe they're still looking. More probably, they're not.

AP/WIDE WORLD

# ⊨ HOMER BIGART ⊨

## WORLD WAR II · KOREA · VIETNAM

*Homer Bigart was a key transitional figure in the history of war correspondence—a great reporter of "the good war" who set the crucial example for great reporters of the bad war in Vietnam. Though he came of age in the 1920s and '30s, Bigart helped to establish the iconoclasm that transformed American journalism in the 1960s and '70s. His pursuit of facts, his challenge to power, and his opinionated style changed the standards by which major reporters were judged. And he wrote spare, vivid prose that deserves to be reread and emulated.*

*Born in 1907, he went to work for the* New York Herald Tribune *as a copy boy in 1927. Chubby and stuttering, he was regarded as dubious reporter material, but he finally won a promotion after five years. He covered the usual run of city and state stories until, in 1943, at thirty-five, he was sent overseas. He reported from London, North*

*Africa, Italy, France, the Pacific, and Japan, where he toured the ruins of Hiroshima. He won his first Pulitzer Prize for his coverage of the Pacific war, though many thought his reporting from Italy, especially the Allied attack on Anzio, had been even better. He wrote about great events of the war's aftermath—including the Jewish campaign against British authority in pre-Israel Palestine and the trial of Adolf Eichmann in 1961—and was widely regarded as the leading chronicler of the war in Korea, where he shared a second Pulitzer with five colleagues, including his detested arch-rival, Marguerite Higgins.*

*Bigart visited Vietnam three times for the* Herald Tribune—*in 1945, 1950, and 1953—each time writing about the increasingly dismal prospects of France's effort to maintain its colonial grip on Indochina. In 1955 he moved from the* Herald Tribune *to the* New York Times. *With reluctance, he agreed to another posting to Vietnam in 1962. "I've applied to be shot at," he wrote in a letter, "but getting the necessary security clearance from U.S. and Vietnamese propaganda engineers takes time." A cold skepticism toward the U.S. Mission—the combined title of the U.S. embassy and military command in Saigon— pervaded his dispatches and influenced rising young colleagues, including Neil Sheehan of United Press International (later of the* Times*), Malcolm Browne of the Associated Press (later of the* Times, *too), and David Halberstam, who succeeded Bigart as the* Times*'s representative in Saigon. Bigart detested Vietnam—the place and the war—and departed after only six months, though not soon enough for the government of South Vietnam, the U.S. contingent in Saigon, or the Kennedy White House.*

*For ten years more he covered events at home, including the civil rights movement and the 1971 trial of Lieutenant William Calley for directing the massacre of Vietnamese civilians at My Lai. Bigart retired from the* Times *in 1972 and died in 1991.*

*There is no biography of Bigart, but his colleague and friend Betsy Wade, an editor at the* Times, *collected some fifty of his dispatches in* Forward Positions: The War Correspondence of Homer Bigart.

*Wade comments here on Bigart's career, as do several colleagues—*
*Walter Cronkite, Andy Rooney, Malcolm Browne, and David Halber-*
*stam.*

———

BETSY WADE: He was born in a town near the coal area of Penn-
sylvania called Hawley. His upbringing was extremely ordinary for
the times. His father was a sweater manufacturer. His mother stayed
at home to watch after Homer and his sister. [After high school, he
went to Carnegie Tech, later Carnegie-Mellon,] with the intention
of becoming an architect. He always told the story that they discovered he couldn't draw and told him to try something else. He
went to New York, got himself a place to live, and got a job at the
*New York Herald Tribune.* He was a copy boy at night and he went
to NYU, studying journalism in a sporadic way. When the stock
market crashed [in 1929], he had to send money home, so he worked
his way up to a full-time job.

These days, the notion of a copy boy's life is as remote as a mule
driver's life. The newspaper city rooms were reasonably large, if
they could afford the space; you can see some of this in the old
newspaper movies, *His Girl Friday,* and the earlier versions of *The
Front Page.* Particularly at a morning newspaper, it got intense in the
evening as the deadline approached at nine or ten o'clock, and things
had to get from one place to the other in the newsroom, especially
if a reporter was writing in what they called "takes," meaning one
piece of paper at a time. They would cry "Copy!" or "Boy!" and
hold the paper up. And [a copy boy] would take it out of their hand
and carry it to the editor, where it was to be looked at or edited or
further processed and then passed on to the composing room, where
it was cast in metal slugs to go [into] page forms. There was an
almost endless need for copy boys on many shifts. During World
War II, there came to be some copy girls, but this was relatively
rare because it was thought to be a hazardous life. The language

was terrible and the verbal abuse was frightful. So you had young people like Homer running back and forth across the city room carrying pieces of copy—and going out to get coffee, taking shoes out to be shined, buying gifts. You could learn a lot.

He became head copy boy, but he had an almost disabling stammer, which made people very doubtful that he could possibly become a reporter. They didn't know how a young man with this kind of difficulty was going to be able to handle it. He was a tough person and sometimes he could be very rugged, particularly when people were difficult or what he believed to be stupid. But I don't think that he was ever mean; I don't think he had a mean bone in his body.

———

*While a copy boy, Bigart tried to earn points toward a promotion by covering stories that regular reporters avoided, including endless church sermons. Even after he was named a reporter in 1932, at the age of twenty-five, he lacked the experience to be assigned to a regular beat and labored on in byline-less anonymity for years.*

———

BETSY WADE: The thing most reporters did not want to do was cover the Sunday morning sermons—to go find out what the Reverend Doctor Whoever was telling the believers when they turned up at 9 o'clock, 10 o'clock, or 11 o'clock. These were important stories in the newspapers of the day, but they were at an inconvenient time on a very inconvenient day, so you found the beginners doing those. Homer did many, many Sunday morning sermons. He covered a lot of night meetings. He was sent down to Princeton to cover the Triangle Club show. By and large, these were anonymous stories with no bylines. He got his first byline in 1940 on a story of the St. Patrick's Day parade, which is a classical tour de force that many reporters have done.

Homer began his interviews in the office. It was simply phenomenal how this man performed. Nothing he ever did, I think, was he unprepared for. As a questioner, according to those who competed against him, he was genuinely impossible. He asked the same questions over and over again because he wasn't satisfied he'd gotten the full answer. He very frequently asked questions like, "Mr. Mayor, how far does your jurisdiction extend?" Questions that most reporters considered embarrassingly obvious.

———

*Describing this technique, a competitor once imagined a group of reporters at a crime scene where a dead man had been found with a knife sticking out of his back. As others would ask the police about suspects and arrests, this fantasy went, Bigart asked, "Cause of death?" and the answer was, "Heart attack." The lesson to reporters was: Never assume. Betsy Wade told of a time during the civil rights movement when the* New York Times *reporter Joseph Lelyveld encountered evidence of Bigart's approach to fact-gathering, which colleagues and competitors came to call "Homer's All-American Dummy Act." Lelyveld was speaking to an official in a southern town whom Bigart had interviewed a few days earlier.*

———

BETSY WADE: The official said, "You know, we had a guy down here last week who said he was from the *New York Times*. But he couldn't have been. He didn't know anything. I had to explain everything to him." And, of course, that was Homer. He didn't know anything; he knew a lot. He knew a lot more than others because he'd done his research. But he also kept asking questions, and to the extent that any of us is able to emulate Homer, we have what he had—the ability always to find something unexpected. As long as somebody was asking questions, a news conference generally did not break up. But part of Homer's gift was his willingness to be unpopular or difficult, or just to keep at it and get it. He wasn't there to win a popularity contest with his fellow workers.

DAVID HALBERSTAM: Homer tried to come on as a lowbrow, but there was a very high intellectual quality to his work. He was extraordinarily sophisticated, and he disguised that sophistication as well as he could. He learned how to use the stutter to his advantage. These innocent public officials would think, "Oh, I've got to help this poor, dear man," and they would pour out all kinds of stuff.

ANDY ROONEY: Homer tended to get more out of the people he was interviewing than the rest of us did because somehow he h-he h-had s-s-such a h-h-hard time getting a q-question out that they were effusive in their reply and gave him more than they would give with the rest of us. It was interesting that it worked to his advantage.

BETSY WADE: He typed the same way he spoke. He would keep hitting the space bar while he waited for the word to come, so you had big gaps between the words, and, of course, strikeovers. Many reporters did not like strikeovers in the days of the typewriter. But Homer never worried about strikeovers and he would just go X X X down a line if he didn't like it, and keep on going. Under the circumstances, it was a good skill. A compulsive typist is not going to do well in the field.

He wrote with difficulty. When you were editing his copy, you could tell how much difficulty because of the spaces between the words. They just got wider and wider while he was thinking. And he was very slow. Harrison Salisbury [then a major figure at United Press, later at the *New York Times*], who first encountered him in London during World War II, said he saw him sitting in magisterial isolation when the other correspondents had finished and gone out to drink. Homer was still there, poking away at it because he wasn't satisfied with what he'd done. And the way the clock goes—with five hours or six hours between London and New York—he had enough time to do that kind of thing.

His vocabulary was rich. When he wrote, he used words that really startled copy editors, and there was frequently a debate about whether the word should be left in or taken out, whether it was too exotic for people to follow.

DAVID HALBERSTAM: One of the reasons that Homer was so good was that he wrote so well. He wrote with a piercing simplicity, and I say that with great admiration. His words were really very precisely chosen. The sentences were simple, but the effect was powerful and understated.

One of the other reasons he was so good was that he was not, as so many journalists are, a morally neutral man. I think he thought—and he never would have expressed this, because he was very careful about being categorized ideologically—that the world was a place where a lot of people did a lot of cruel things, and that a real journalist's job was to cast some light on that cruelty. Once in a while, you would get a flash of rage in one of his stories, and it was really a reflection of the moral judgment of a man who had devoted his life, involuntarily, to seeing much of the human race at its very worst.

Unlike most legends, he was everything he was supposed to be. He was the prototype reporter's reporter.

———

*Early in 1943, Bigart became, with Walter Cronkite and Andy Rooney, one of the so-called Writing 69th—the small group of correspondents chosen as the first to accompany U.S. airmen on a bombing mission over Nazi-occupied Europe. The raid, scheduled for Bremen, was diverted by weather to Wilhelmshaven. A B-24 Liberator carrying Rob-*

*ert Post of the* New York Times *was shot down, killing all aboard. Bigart's devotion to an understated style of description became evident that day to Cronkite.*

———

WALTER CRONKITE: When we had landed at our base, my dear friend Homer Bigart was with me. Homer was a purist about writing, and a very good writer. He avoided the headline-type writing that we were accustomed to in the wire services.

BETSY WADE: Here the men are, riding back from the airfield, all jangled nerves, all upset, and they're saying, "What are you going to do? What are you going to write?"

WALTER CRONKITE: Homer said, "W-w-w-what's g-g-going to be your-your-your l-lead?" I said I had this in my mind: "I've just returned from a suburb of hell, a hell at seventeen thousand feet, a hell of falling bombs, of burning bombers," and so forth.

Homer looked at me and said, "Y-y-y-you w-w-w-wouldn't."

———

*Bigart's own report, reprinted in Wade's* Forward Positions, *is quite lacking in Cronkite's wire-service melodrama. It carried this lead: "Our target was Wilhelmshaven. We struck at Führer Adolf Hitler's North Sea base from the southwest after stoogeing around over a particularly hot corner of the Third Reich for what seemed like a small eternity." A week later, in a first-person follow-up story in the* Herald Tribune, *Bigart reflected on the difficulty a correspondent faced in assessing any action in which "your own neck was directly involved." Without naming his friend Cronkite, whose account of the raid, lead and all, had appeared in the rival* New York Times, *Bigart had a bit of fun at his expense.*

*Having survived exposure to danger in battle, Bigart said, "You are apt to feel you had a ringside seat at the most crucial engagement since Waterloo or that final Yankee-Cardinal game at the Stadium. This is known as the 'I have just returned from a suburb of hell' reaction. To relieve this condition, it is necessary for the patient to hurl himself at the nearest typewriter, rap out a tingling yarn of a flak-filled heaven, of epic dog fights and derring-do.... You want to write about raging fires, shattering explosions and rivers of German blood."*

*But after a day or two, Bigart said, he had realized that no reporter in a bomber under attack—at least, not a neophyte like himself—had anywhere near the time and presence of mind to really see, much less evaluate, the damage a bombing raid had done. Thus he learned "a truth that should be communicated to every student of journalism: A good deal of experience is needed to qualify as a competent aerial observer." Or, he might have added, as a competent observer of any other slice of the complex reality that all reporters must interpret.*

———

BETSY WADE: Of Homer's many achievements, I think his coverage of Italy is the thing that people go back to and read most often. His Italian correspondence is so close to the ground. After Sicily, he was sent up to Anzio—to this tiny beachhead with their backs to the water and the Germans ahead of them—and he was there for ninety days. A bombshell landed in his bathtub. Almost everything he did was on foot, so that when they came to trip wires or booby traps that had been left behind by the retreating Germans, Homer was the one in several cases who saw it. He referred to "the unregistered guest" in the hotel in a town that they came into, and this was a German tank that had been left in the middle of the hotel lobby. All of these things were intimate. And Homer's ability to do what Ernie Pyle was so good at doing as he was moving along—that is, to get the names of the soldiers and get their hometowns—was wonderfully rich. You saw these kids from Iowa and Michigan and hundreds of other places struggling their way north through Italy and not talking about anything flying overhead or dropping bombs from remote points. These were people who were making their way through Italy inch by inch in pursuit of a terribly bloody, mean, rotten war.

I think there was a great difference between [Pyle's work and Bigart's]. I think Pyle found a particular specialty at which no one could match him, and that was the life of the dogface. He went through everything from what it smells like to what kind of food they were getting to how they died, and he built, I think, a lasting memorial for a lot of people who otherwise would have had nothing. Homer encompassed other aspects of the war correspondent. Homer wasn't afraid to take on the military planners. He correctly called the Anzio campaign a disaster. He said [the soldiers at Anzio] were ill-equipped; they weren't prepared to stay there; they couldn't handle it. And at one point, the British general who was in charge of this really let loose, denouncing the American correspondents for hurting morale, for damaging the war effort. What Homer was doing was what he did until the very end of his life. He was telling the truth as he saw it. He honestly believed that the American people had a right to know if things were going badly.

When Homer was sent off to cover the trial [in Israel] of Adolf Eichmann [the Nazi SS officer who had administered the extermination of European Jews], he didn't know how he was going to cover it, because he always had to have an underdog and there didn't seem to be a living underdog at the trial. As it turned out, there were a number of underdogs, of the most unbelievable clearness of memory, who testified in the Eichmann trial, and Homer wrote about this with a vividness that is, I think, unparalleled.

Everywhere, [Bigart wrote about] the people who were getting pushed around—the small people who were not figured into the grand scheme of things. And the people that Homer did not like were oppressors or bigots. When Homer covered any number of civil rights campaigns in the United States, he had no trouble at all understanding what he was doing, because he knew who the underdog was. He covered disastrous human events. And because he needed an underdog and because that's what a newspaper is built out of, he was a master at this kind of thing. He could almost always find people in a town who had suffered at the hands of some terrible person. War was simply an elaboration of that. Death, pain, wounds, loss—I think these were part of the basic human proportions that Homer saw before him each time he went out.

Homer always went as far forward as you could go. But he did not—urgently did not—want to get killed. There is a story of Homer and a number of other correspondents driving along in a jeep and a bomb hits the road immediately in front of them. And the driver freezes and says, "Where should I go?" And Homer says, "Ahead." And indeed, another bomb drops back where they had been. So they go ahead.

But he was careful. He wasn't reckless. He didn't want to be a dead hero. He wanted to be a live correspondent. And I think this is what brought the terrible, terrible dispute between Homer and Marguerite Higgins, both of whom were working for the *Herald Tribune* during the Korean War.

———

*Higgins had been a prominent correspondent in World War II. She was extremely aggressive and daring. In spite of that trait, or perhaps in part because of it, many other reporters came to loathe her. A male colleague on the* Herald Tribune *called her "a dangerous, venomous bitch, and a bad reporter," while a female biographer summed up her reporting technique as "Big blue eyes, a high-pitched little girl's voice, and sex appeal....As a last resort, she used her head." In Korea, Higgins and Bigart competed for front-page space in the* Herald Tribune *every day.*

———

BETSY WADE: They were pushing each other so hard that Homer felt, very frequently, that he was going to get himself killed trying to stay ahead of, or equal to, Marguerite, who was a much greater risk taker than he was. The *Herald Tribune* was in an unparalleled position. It had two absolutely top correspondents, one of whom [Bigart] had already won a Pulitzer Prize. They were beating up on each other and trying to outdo each other with their dispatches. So all the *Herald Tribune* had to do was sit there in New York and just rake in these wonderful stories and decide how to play them on page one. What was happening out in the field was bitter and harsh, because Homer was very, very sure that if Marguerite could cause him to endanger himself and get himself killed, she would. That would be her way out of the competition.

———

*Higgins's reports from Korea tended toward the gung-ho style and the hero worship that made Bigart flinch. His horror of Higgins became legendary. When he was told that Higgins and her husband had a new baby, he was reported to have said either "Well, did she eat it?" or "Wonderful, who's the mother?" When Betsy Wade later asked Bigart which of the two remarks he actually had made, he said "Yes."*

———

BETSY WADE: I think the fact that Marguerite was a woman in the field was about 90 percent responsible for his attitude. The other 10 percent was that she liked the generals. She had a feeling that they were a part of the story that deserved more of the coverage.

After it was all over and they had shared a Pulitzer Prize, along with others, for their work in Korea, Homer said that he had been terribly unfair and needlessly cruel to Marguerite Higgins, who, after all, was a good, pushy correspondent, which is what a corre-

spondent should be. And the day at the *Times* when the ne[
Higgins's death [in 1966] of [the tropical disease] leishma[
came, about four of the young correspondents descended upon ..v-
mer [and asked for his comment]. He said, "You can't say anything
about somebody who died so terribly." In later years, in his interviews, he acknowledged his anxieties and his fears had led him to
make a lot of mistakes, including an effort at one point to get Marguerite Higgins recalled on the ground that she was behaving in an
unseemly fashion. The tales of Marguerite Higgins and Homer Bigart are legion. I'm sorry they're all there, but they're there, and
probably some of them are even true.

I think Homer's six months in Vietnam is one of the most important
legacies he has left younger correspondents, and to ones, I suppose,
who haven't been born yet. I hope they will find a way to do what
he did.

[Before he left the United States for South Vietnam in 1962] we
were having dinner one time and he said, "Well, they're bastards,
but they're our bastards." He believed that before he went there.
When he came back, I don't think he believed any longer that they
were *our* bastards. I think he believed that the United States was
involved in a long-term, failing mission.

MALCOLM BROWNE: Those of us who were already in Saigon at the
time Homer Bigart arrived in 1962 knew all about him—even those
of us who had never met him—because he was a legend. He was
much fatter than I imagined him to be. He had a speech impediment
that I hadn't known about. He also was an impeccable dresser, at least
whenever he was dining in one of the restaurants with friends or with
news contacts. He would dress in a dark blue suit. On operations,
he finally went to the length of buying himself an olive drab jacket.

Actually, a reputation as vast as Homer's is a tremendous asset
when you're trying to wiggle your way into some situation where

you're trying to beat out your competitors. I remembered that he infuriated Roy Essoyan of the Associated Press by getting in ahead of him on one of the first helicopter operations in late 1962 or early 1963. Roy had been working on this for a long time—also a seasoned correspondent, brought up in China, trilingual, really a legendary correspondent himself—but Homer got the best of him.

I was often lucky enough to find myself working the same stories he was. Although we were technically competitors, we felt comfortable in each other's company, and I certainly gained from watching him in action.

Homer hated Vietnam. He never made any bones about it. It was a country that he despised because of the essential falsity of its protocol. You could go talk to some senior general and come away feeling that you'd probably learned a lot and that he was being very kind and nice to you, when in fact he was sabotaging you with false information. Homer hated that. He hated deception. And Vietnam was nothing if not deceptive. I think every American leader who ever passed through there, including all the American ambassadors during the war years, ended with the conclusion that you cannot trust the Vietnamese under any circumstances, even under the best circumstances. You could if you knew their game. That's the thing. You had to penetrate this social way in which everything is deception, but it is expected that you will see through the deception, and therefore it's fair game.

BETSY WADE: In the six months that he was there, Homer was absent as much as he was present [for the daily press briefings by U.S. officials] because that barely interested him at all. He was finding doctors doing heroic work. He was finding quasi-military organizations created by the Vietnamese themselves. He was off to Da Nang. He was always moving around and finding things; he was interviewing people, looking at how things went.

Homer was extremely dubious about everything that was going

on. The United States was fighting a guerrilla war with techniques that, in his view, had worked pretty well in Italy [in World War II] but were certainly not going to work well in the jungles of Vietnam. It was perfectly clear to him that the [South] Vietnamese were not fighting well, that they didn't want to fight, that this was a war that seemed extremely undesirable from a U.S. standpoint.

DAVID HALBERSTAM: He'd seen *Indochine One* and I don't think he had any taste for *Indochine Two*. He was shrewd. He knew much more than we did, in a historical sense. He knew what the outcome was going to be—that it was going to be dirty and messy, and other people's kids were going to get killed; that the press was going to get whacked for doing its job; that it was going to be a mean and ugly time, ending in some kind of defeat. And I don't think he wanted any part of it. His greatest pleasure every day was X-ing out one more day on the calendar.

There's a terrific story, a very early story, when the American helicopters had first come into the country. This was going to be the new, high-technology answer to going after the VC [Vietcong]. So Homer goes down to Mytho with this twenty-five-year-old kid, Neil Sheehan [then of United Press International, later of the *New York Times*]. And oh, boy, the Americans are really excited: "Now we can really chase them." The helicopters were these god-awful old CH-21s left over from the Korean War that looked like flying locusts. But this was going to be three days of famous victories, and the first day, there was a sort of medium-sized victory. Then, the second day, there's a classic pillow-punching operation where [the South Vietnamese Army] deliberately signaled that they were coming so the VC could avoid contact. And the same thing the third day.

So the two of them are driving back to Saigon and Neil is sitting there and he's muttering, because a UPI guy is not supposed to leave the office much and three days is a big investment. He's muttering away and Homer says, "Mr. Sheehan, wh-wh-what's the m-matter?" And Neil says, "You know, three days wasted and no story—waste of time." And Homer says, "M-Mr. Sh-Sheehan, there is a s-story. It doesn't work. That's your story."

That was it. He understood the backdrop of the French-Indochina War. I think he understood their political muscle—the VC and later the NVA [Army of North Vietnam] had absolute political superiority and we had absolute military superiority. We would win any set-piece battle, but they would go back at night and keep recruiting. And he understood that because he had the history. He'd been there. He had the advantage you get for being older— and very good.

BETSY WADE: I think my favorite image of Homer Bigart was standing at a wretched bar called Gough's, which [disappeared] under the gentrification of Times Square. Bleeck's, which was the *Herald Tribune* bar, was distinguished and beautiful and had been a speakeasy. Gough's was the *Times*'s bar, and it was neither distinguished nor beautiful. But Homer liked Gough's. He said, "Gough's saloon is indeed a low place, but newspapering is a low profession."

One night before he left town for an overseas assignment, we closed three bars in Times Square, which was a little harder to do in those days. We staggered into the street after this battle with Gough's and Sardi's and the Blue Ribbon, and a little snow was beginning to fall in Times Square, and Homer said, "New York is never so beautiful as when you're leaving in six hours." And that was a true gift.

Wanting to get the story, as Homer always did—being hungry— is the most important thing to have, to begin with. There will be a lot of college-educated people covering extremely complicated issues—financial issues, the world market, technology, all of these things. But it will be wanting the story that will move them and make them great.

In an offhanded way, Homer said once, "I think I'm a pacifist."

He was not a war lover, and it's important to understand that for people who are war lovers, being a foreign correspondent, of course, is a life in paradise. It makes aspects of the Marquis de Sade look suitable for Saturday afternoon entertainment. But he didn't like it. He didn't like being uncomfortable. He didn't like being cold. He liked decent food. He liked to have a drink. He loved his wives— most particularly his last wife [the children's author Else Holmelund Minarik]—and he liked a comfortable life.

DAVID HALBERSTAM: I remember one time in New York when Neil [Sheehan] and I had come back from Vietnam, and we went out to dinner with him. He'd just been to see *Oh, What a Lovely War,* which is an anti–World War I movie. We got back to his apartment and he started playing the record of it, and he started singing the songs. Neil and I looked at each other, and there was this epiphany. We suddenly thought, "Homer Bigart, this famous war correspondent, whom we revered so much and had covered all the worst things of the twentieth century, hated war. This man that had this great reputation for being so brave had been doing this because he really hated what he saw."

BETSY WADE: Trying to discuss how people outside of the news business should remember Homer is extremely complicated. It's like saying, "How do we remember a flower that blooms only once a year?" Here was a man who never wrote a book; who wrote about ten magazine articles, at best; whose entire life's work was published in a newspaper, which goes to nothing pretty quickly, and even the microfilm is not easy to get at.

He provided us with a transitory, essential element at the time he was doing it. Trying to preserve this kind of work is extremely difficult because you have to surround it with a context. Perhaps, again, it's like someone who grows wonderful orchids. You have to see the orchid while it's there.

Why should we care about war correspondents as people? I think because they are not machines. I watch machines work in this day and age and it's hard to tell what was written ten years ago from what's written today. These were not machines. These were human beings whose perceptions shaped a great deal of what we understood, whose willingness to risk themselves—for the public's need to know and for their own glory and because they loved it—is invaluable to us.

FOR FURTHER READING:

Betsy Wade, ed., *Forward Positions: The War Correspondence of Homer Bigart* (University of Arkansas Press, 1992)

# ⊣ MALCOLM W. BROWNE ⊢

## VIETNAM · PERSIAN GULF

*The Associated Press sent Malcolm Browne to Saigon in the fall of 1961, when the American Mission in Vietnam was new. Raised in Greenwich Village in the 1930s and '40s by an architect father and a Quaker mother, Browne attended Swarthmore College and chose a career in chemistry. But the draft took him to postwar Korea, where he learned journalism on the staff of the Army daily, the* Stars and Stripes. *At the age of thirty, after AP assignments abroad and at home, he sought the wire service's post in Saigon.*

*In the Republic of South Vietnam, the United States was supporting the government of an odd and insular Catholic intellectual, Ngo Dinh Diem, as a bulwark against Communist insurgents based in North Vietnam and led by Ho Chi Minh. With lean stories that reported the facts as they unfolded before his eyes, Browne soon found himself at*

*loggerheads with Diem's corrupt government and his bizarre relatives,*
*who wielded much of the power in Saigon. Vietnam became the crucible*
*of his adult life, the place where he met his wife—a controversial*
*official in the Diem regime—and won the Pulitzer Prize. For the AP,*
*ABC News, and the* New York Times, *he covered the story of the*
*American war for various periods from beginning to end.*

*After Vietnam, Browne became a distinguished science reporter, both*
*at the* Times *and at* Discover *magazine. But in 1991, he returned*
*to war reporting, covering the Persian Gulf War for the* Times.

———

For me, getting to Saigon was the realization of a dream. Back in
the days when I worked in a laboratory, I used to analyze cassia
bark, which is like cinnamon. It had the most wonderful smell, and
I associated that with the beautiful pictures I'd seen of lovely girls
in conical hats in Saigon. To a very large extent, that sort of am-
bience prevailed, even after the war began to heat up. In the early
days, it was a mix of the really beautiful and exotic with sheer
horror. And for me, that was very congenial.

I came because in 1961 Indochina had suddenly become page
one news. I was working for the Associated Press in Baltimore at
the time, and there was a tremendous incentive for me to go to
Vietnam and try to make a name for myself as a war correspondent.
I had covered some wars before—the Cuban revolution and things
like that—but this was really large-scale, and I thought it would be
a fascinating experience. I was just overjoyed when the phone call
came from my boss in New York, Wes Gallagher, who was an old
warhorse himself, saying, "Can you get to Saigon in about three
days?"

I came from a very different background from that of most of
my colleagues. I was not a born journalist. I was a born chemist. I
was diverted away from the laboratory by a succession of events—
being drafted and sent to Korea, mainly. But I think I was always

guided in my thinking about the war as if I were a chemist
than a correspondent. I've never had much respect for news c
spondents. In fact, I was not a great newspaper reader as a k.u. I
read papers every now and then, but I never took them seriously.
So when I got to Saigon, I was resolved not to treat this as journalism but as a piece of observation that should be as accurate and
as telling as possible, looking for the truth behind the truth.

I had no interest in becoming a public figure, nor did I entertain
any ideas of prizes. It seemed to me that the purpose of journalism
was to enjoy the maximum variety of experience that I could sum-
mon from this wonderful environment—the world around me. And
I was aware that war had produced some of the most dramatic
situations there are. There's horror—there's no question about that.
There's the tension of not knowing whether you're going to be
killed in the next assault. But there's also this strange feeling of
having your life on the line—of knowing you could get killed but
you're somehow making it. And there's the tremendous feeling of
exhilaration when you emerge from a battle and find yourself reasonably unscathed. War is not only fun, it's high drama—unless, of
course, you sustain personal loss. It is a greater experience than
anything you can have in the theater, or in the opera, or in a Greek
tragedy. Besides the horror, war includes all of these things.

The State Department, the CIA, the Defense Intelligence Agency,
the Pentagon—everybody who was involved in Vietnam, either
openly or covertly, regarded it as a piece of theater in which one
of the primary objects was to impress the press corps with the rightness of the cause, the cleverness and courage of the people carrying
it out, and with all the good things they were doing. To this end,
the Mission brought in a public relations firm whose job it was to
hold the hands of all the newsmen in Saigon and at the same time
make sure they got no information about anything of any conceivable use. It was obvious from the first two days after I arrived in

Saigon that this flimflam was a very explicit campaign to mislead the press in Vietnam.

From the very outset, both sides recognized that this was, more than anything else, a political war. In Washington, the whole trick was to persuade the American public that this was a good war, a war worth fighting. The propaganda on the [North Vietnamese] side was, of course, aimed at explaining how American airplanes were bombing and strafing innocent villagers and doing the kind of thing that sometimes happens in the reality of war. So there were two essentially different worldviews.

The correspondents in Saigon were going out in the field every day, talking to people, seeing what was happening, seeing that the war was not only being lost, but that it was probably right to be lost, that there were lots of good reasons why Americans shouldn't be there in the first place, because it was essentially a civil war between north and south, to put it as simply as possible.

————

*In 1961, the U.S. State Department had sent a secret cable to Saigon, instructing officials that in their dealings with the press, they should emphasize that the war was being fought by the South Vietnamese. "It is not...in our interest," the cable said, "to have stories indicating that Americans are leading and directing combat missions."*

————

It was made very clear that the United States would never send combatants to Vietnam, but simply advisers and assistants. For me, the moment of truth occurred about a week after I arrived in Vietnam, when I took a car up to the main military airport, about twenty-five miles from Saigon. I was stopped at the gate, couldn't get in. But I did see some T-28s taxiing. I noticed that in one of the T-28s that was taxiing near the perimeter fence, there were two people, as usual, but the guy in the front had blue eyes and blond hair, and the guy in the back was obviously an Asian. Now, this suggested that the doctrine that Americans were there only to advise and not to fight was simply not true. Furthermore, there were weapons in the pods of this aircraft. It wasn't a training mission. You could see from the smoke stains that it had just been in action. I took some pictures. The pictures were then confiscated by military police.

This was a symptom of what was going on that colored everything that came after. Everything we were being told was, if not a total lie, at least a distortion of the truth. One morning we were having our croissants and we noticed that down at the end of the street there was an aircraft carrier. This was something you didn't ordinarily see along Saigon's main street. So those of us who spotted it scampered over to see. There it was, a gigantic aircraft carrier. The first thing we did was to try to find an American who could speak to this issue of what was happening to disturb our breakfast. And the response at the U.S. Information Agency was, "Aircraft carrier? What aircraft carrier? I don't see anything."

And that was, of course, typical. I mean, it was tongue-in-cheek, but it was also deadly serious, because the idea was that no information would be given to the intrusive American press about what was essentially a semiclandestine operation, even though it was an aircraft carrier they were trying to hide. This kind of thing happened again and again.

The military realized perfectly well that the correspondents there were too smart not to see through all this nonsense. But the point is that they got out their word, and their word went back home to Washington, and Washington was where the congressmen were, and the policymakers and all the people who really count— including the Washington press corps. That's what motivated this continuing charade.

For the most part, the Washington press corps never went anywhere but Washington. I think that may have changed somewhat now, but certainly in the days of the Vietnam War, it was a very homebound press corps who would attend the State Department and other Washington briefings and then write their copy as performing seals. There were some notable failures of journalism among them. I would have to count Joseph Alsop as among the most off-base. Alsop had had some experience in Indochina. He'd covered the fall of China itself, and he'd been in Hanoi during the first Indochina war. He felt that it was enough for him to revisit Saigon about once every six months or so, debrief the local correspondents, including myself, and write a long tale about it which basically reflected what Washington had been saying all along. There was another correspondent—I won't mention his name in deference to his memory—who wrote a long story saying no coup would occur in Saigon. It was published by his newspaper, the *Chicago Daily News*, on the very day that Ngo Dinh Diem was overthrown in a coup.

———

*Alsop and other journalists close to the Kennedy administration soon targeted Browne and like-minded skeptics in Saigon as ambitious troublemakers who were endangering the American Mission. Chief among the critics was Marguerite Higgins, the swashbuckling star of the* New York Herald Tribune, *who had dueled with Homer Bigart in Korea.*

———

Maggie was married to an Air Force general, and was very much "on the team," as Admiral [Harry D.] Felt used to call it. Maggie was a very attractive woman in lots of ways, but she was, I think, guided wholly by ideology in her reporting. She was very much a World War II type of reporter of the would-be Ernie Pyle type—being one with the Marines in all their travails and never having anything nasty to say about the cause.

Maggie and I were in Cambodia at the same time, and I tried

inviting her to a riverside restaurant that I liked very much. We went there and chatted, and I made it plain to her that I was hoping we could bury the hatchet—that this kind of wrangling was pointless. But in the course of the dinner, which consisted mainly of Cambodian soup—a noodle soup that ordinarily is eaten with a big spoon and a pair of chopsticks—I discovered to my great surprise that in all her years in Korea and China and Indochina, Maggie had never learned how to handle chopsticks. She actually pulled the noodles out with one hand in order to get hold of them, to the embarrassment of lots of people who were watching. This is nothing against her, but to me it illustrated the almost total lack of communication she'd had with the cultural background of the region in which she was working and observing. This always seemed to me one of the most important things a correspondent should master— some knowledge of how things are done in a nation you're trying to cover.

She never had anything against me except that I was one of the enemy, in her eyes. Her main attack, I think, was on David Halberstam, whom she regarded as the lowest form of life. She took the line that was adopted by *Time* magazine and the *Chicago Tribune* and various other right-wing newspapers and organizations—that essentially the Young Turks were trying to make a name for themselves at the expense of their nation, that they were traitors to their nation's cause, that they were interested in their own aggrandizement and not in winning the war. That was essentially her line—and furthermore that the war was being won and that her great and dear friend Ngo Dinh Diem and his family were doing just the right things, as were the many Americans who supported him.

———

*Browne, Bigart, Neil Sheehan of UPI, Halberstam (Bigart's successor at the* Times*), Charles Mohr of* Time, *and Peter Arnett of AP con-*

*stituted a cadre whose reporting on the Diem regime was embarrassing to the Kennedy administration, which struck back with efforts to have the correspondents denigrated, muzzled, or transferred.*

———

They attempted to portray the Saigon press corps as a bunch of luxury-loving people who spent all their time at the bar in the Caravelle Hotel, dreaming up stories that they'd force on the American public. Otto Fuerbringer, the managing editor of *Time* magazine, liked this approach and devoted several of his "Press" pages to blistering attacks on the young correspondents in Saigon who were doing all these terrible things. Charlie Mohr, who was *Time's* correspondent at the time, was so infuriated by this distortion that he quit, which was a very courageous thing to do. Many months later, he joined the *New York Times,* which supported him.

That was the kind of approach that was taken. The government would not directly condemn a correspondent for his or her story, but would pass the word among the true believers and friends, like Joseph Alsop and Otto Fuerbringer, who in turn would put out their point of view in their newspapers or magazines. It was a very underhanded way of going about it.

I remember that we were told what was in the [*Time*] article by various people who had read it. We didn't hold any protest meetings or anything like that, but we were obviously greatly embittered. I even talked about suing *Time.* Finally, in the absence of anything else to do, I hung up a quote from John Lennon of the Beatles that said, "Our fans don't read *Time* magazine anyway." As we turned out to be more and more right, and our detractors more and more wrong, the balance of influence tended to shift. At a certain point, I think that our readers were believing us and not what was coming out of Washington.

• • •

I felt fully supported by my own organization. The AP under Wes Gallagher [who had covered World War II] was a tower of strength. Wes had reason to be particularly grateful to General [William] Westmoreland for services rendered in the past. Westmoreland had saved his life in World War II by pulling Wes out of a burning jeep. Now, one would expect that after that experience, Gallagher would have become a performing seal when confronted with people like Westmoreland in Vietnam. He came out to Saigon and I took him on a tour of the Mekong Delta and various other places that were being hotly contested; showed him how hamlets were controlled by the good guys in the daytime but were completely under Vietcong control at night; how most of the figures coming out of official sources—showing how well we were doing, how many weapons captured—were just nonsense. By the end of that visit, Wes was a true believer and a supporter of his reporters in Vietnam.

As the military became more used to correspondents being around and not dynamiting the headquarters, we did gradually get more access to some of these things. Before anybody really knew that helicopters were in combat in Vietnam, David Halberstam and Neil Sheehan and I were among the very first to go out on helicopter missions. I remember spending Christmas Eve 1961 at the Ranger camp in which Special Forces troops were training Cambodian Rangers—Cambodians in Vietnam, because the Vietnamese government trusted Cambodians in sensitive jobs like that more than they did their own people. It was a very interesting night. The Americans would fire star shells from their mortars to celebrate Christmas Eve, and the Vietcong a hundred yards away would fire tracers up to meet the star shells, and it was one big happy family— until the following day, when all slaughter broke loose.

Neither the Pentagon nor the State Department ever completely excluded us from things that were going on. They eventually became somewhat more tolerant of our operations. They never formally censored our dispatches, but what they did do was to operate a liaison with the South Vietnamese authorities that was, in effect, censorship. They would warn the Vietnamese telegraph office that some sensitive dispatches were coming through that they didn't really like. So these dispatches got mysteriously lost and delayed for days and days at a time. So in fact there *was* censorship, but it was carried out by Vietnamese authorities. That was the beginning of a long battle—censorship on the part of the Vietnamese government and ways of circumventing censorship on the part of the foreign correspondents.

———

*In 1963, Browne began to pay close attention to the rising Buddhist opposition to the Diem regime. Monks and nuns from Buddhist pagodas staged a series of protests in several cities, including Saigon, and their acts of civil disobedience became increasingly troublesome to Diem and his backers in Washington.*

———

Because of what I knew of the Buddhist tradition in Vietnam, I realized that it had to be taken seriously. So while other correspondents got tired of the endless Buddhist street demonstrations that were going on all that summer, I stuck with them, because I had the sense that sooner or later something would happen. I became a familiar presence at the main pagoda in Saigon. The monks knew that I appreciated their cuisine. We were friendly. One of them was a Yale graduate, as a matter of fact. And I was sincerely interested in what they were doing, quite aside from the news value of it.

One monk in particular would telephone me in advance the night before something was planned. One night he advised me to come to the pagoda at seven the next morning because something very special and important was going to happen. He sent the same message to half a dozen other American correspondents, but they all ignored it. I did not. That was all.

That morning a Buddhist monk went out and sat down in a main intersection in downtown Saigon. Two of his fellow monks poured gasoline over him, and he set himself on fire and died. I was there, the only western correspondent present and taking pictures. I suppose I took six or eight rolls of 35-millimeter film.

It was clearly theater staged by the Buddhists to achieve a certain political end. At the same time, there was a human element to it that was just horrifying, because the sequence of pictures showed the initial shock of the flames touching his face, and so forth. He never cried out or screamed, but you could see from his expression that he was exposed to intense agony, and that he was dying on the spot—and then, in the end, when the body was rigidly burned, they couldn't stuff him into a casket because he was splayed out in all directions. As shock photography goes, it was hard to beat. It's not something that I'm particularly proud of. If one wants to be gruesome about it, it was a very easy sequence of pictures to take. Work is a great panacea for the horrors of that sort of situation, or of a battle, for that matter. I think combat photographers are very conscious of the idea that the real fear comes later, after they get home and develop their film and have a look at what they were through. Then they are aware that they nearly died.

It was a picture that meant many things to many different people and interests. The Chinese and the North Vietnamese regarded it as a wonderful propaganda picture, and of course they labeled it "A Buddhist priest dies to oppose U.S. imperialism and its influence in Vietnam." In the United States, it was regarded as a picture of a martyr who had died for a worthy cause, and therefore other Americans should support the overthrow of an autocratic Catholic government that had been supported by President Kennedy.

I've been asked a couple times whether I could have prevented the suicide. I could not. There was a phalanx of perhaps two hundred monks and nuns who were ready to block me if I tried to move. A couple of them chucked themselves under the wheels of a fire truck that arrived. But in the years since, I've had this searing feeling of perhaps having in some way contributed to the death of a kind old man who probably would not have done what he did—nor would the monks in general have done what they did—if they had not been assured of the presence of a newsman who could convey the images and experience to the outer world. Because that was the whole point—to produce theater of the horrible so striking that the reasons for the demonstrations would become apparent to everyone. And, of course, they did. The following day, President Kennedy had the photograph on his desk, and he called in Henry Cabot Lodge, who was about to leave for Saigon as U.S. ambassador, and told him, in effect, "This sort of thing has got to stop." And that was the beginning of the end of American support for the Ngo Dinh Diem regime.

Usually I was limited to dispatches of about two or three hundred words. This was agony, there's no question about it. This is a major shortcoming of the craft of journalism for everybody, whether they are on television or writing for newspapers. But as Vietnam began to slide onto page one of the newspapers, the constraints on the length of dispatches were lifted. The day that Ngo Dinh Diem was overthrown, Wes Gallagher asked me to write a piece at about three thousand words to summarize the background, and it was duly distributed by the wires.

You were constrained in the kind of material that you could send back. Your editors expected you to handle it much as you would a sports story. There was the running lead story about who won what and which ridge line had been captured and which town had been lost. That's one story. There was a box-score story which gives all the figures on body counts. And then there was the locker room story, with the dying Marine or the soldier who'd been in combat too long and was cracking up. Those three types of stories generally are expected almost every day in a war. They're all misleading because war is not a sport, after all. War depends not necessarily on numbers but on the reality of a situation. It can only be told in the most searching kind of story that requires the length, for example, of a magazine piece in something like the *New Yorker*. To really cover a war requires reflection and introspection as well as the hard facts. Sometimes it can be done in just a sentence or two that bring home the telling reality much better than the fact that we killed five or fifty Vietcong yesterday.

———

*In 1965, Browne left the AP to become a correspondent for ABC News. In 1968 he joined the* New York Times, *for which he continued to write about the war.*

———

I joined ABC in the belief that television was *the* medium—that people really paid attention to television and much less so to newspapers and wire services. So it was in the interest of getting the word across, somehow or other. I was recruited and taken to Mexico City to be launched the same year that Adam West was being launched as Batman on the ABC network. In a taxi on the way to the airport, the news president of ABC gave me the straight poop, which was, in effect, that television is an entertainment medium and you must never forget that—that even in serious things like covering a war, you have to be aware that what people want is not just a lot of dry conversation, but firing and that kind of thing. He said public service requires that there are news programs; otherwise, we wouldn't have news programs; we could run grade Z westerns against each other and do fine.

I went back to Saigon. I covered all kinds of things that were of varying importance and interest. But friction built up between me and management over what deserved to be covered. At one point, I was about to depart for a one-day operation by helicopter to watch a new tactic for moving troops around very rapidly, jumping from one spot to another. I thought it would be useful for us to see whether that was going to work, and I made arrangements to go out with a film crew. When word came from New York that they would prefer me to cover the selection of Miss Saigon—well, it seemed to me just completely wrong, and it was the straw that broke the camel's back. I sent back the film in a can along with my resignation.

I think television had a profound effect on the war. But I would not say, as do some, that the television war was what did in the U.S. effort to win the country. More than anything else, I think the feelings about Vietnam changed monumentally when the body bags began coming home, and most of all when people got bored. After all, it was the longest war we'd ever fought, and somehow it didn't seem to be going anywhere. The American public was promised year after year that "we're almost finished," that "we see the light at the end of the tunnel." And somehow it never came to pass. There was no longer excitement. The days when there were songs about the Green Berets were long past.

Still, the images of body bags and huts being burned down... Morley Safer of CBS was the target of tremendous attacks for filming the torching of a peasant hut with a Zippo lighter. In fact, he's still criticized for that. At a symposium about war at Boston University, I met with senior military officials who were talking about the present day. And, inevitably, Morley came up as "one of the real villains of the Vietnam War." These things die hard. The sons of military officers in Vietnam were still taking up the same cant as to how the press can lose a war. And it's silly.

I think that for all people at war, the important truth is the truth that tells you "we are the good guys and we are winning," regardless of what team you're on. Even the Germans during World War II had this approach. Toward the end of the Vietnam War, it was no longer possible to believe in the goodness and rightness of our cause. But instead of blaming the people who had made that cause, I think the United States tended to blame the messengers—people like myself who had been sending back discouraging tidings of how bad things had been going.

The horrors that television depicted were not even as horrible as they might have been. The My Lai massacre, for example, was not televised. That story had a tremendous impact on many, many Americans. The knowledge that we could be pure, outright bad guys in certain circumstances—it made people doubt the wisdom of the war.

As a nation, we went to Vietnam in hopes of saving it from becoming another domino in the chain of communism across the face of Asia. Yet we discovered that in many cases, we were hurting the Vietnamese people more than helping. And even in helping, we did wrong somehow or other. By supplying Louisiana rice, we managed to make the country almost totally dependent on imported American rice rather than the great crops the country had grown in the past. We were very sincere and very naive people back in the early '60s. We kidded ourselves about the virtue of our cause and the simplicity of human life. And Vietnam never was anything but complicated, fiendishly complicated.

One of the things that we in Vietnam could never really understand was the polarization of the people back home into hawks and doves, because to most of us, there was no such thing as a good guy or a bad guy in Vietnam. It was all shades of gray. I saw atrocities committed by both sides—horrible things, things that haunt my dreams even now, many years later. At the same time, there could be great gentleness and courage. On the final day in Saigon, the end of April in 1975, when the country was in chaos, when people were doing everything they could to escape, these complications and contradictions became more apparent than ever. On the one hand, here were Americans helping to heave would-be refugees over the fence so they could get into helicopters to get out. On the other hand, here were Americans accepting bribes of gold and the favors of women to get police out of the country. A raging corruption. All kinds of cruelty. This inevitable mix of cruelty and warmth and kindness perhaps is characteristic of all wars. But in Vietnam it was particularly apparent. That made it impossible to come away with a feeling that Vietnam was good or Vietnam was bad.

I think a war correspondent should serve much the same role that a laboratory assistant does when he's taking down data from an experiment. I know that many of my colleagues disagree with this, but if he becomes a watchdog, it makes him a partisan of some cause, to expose one side as evil. I think it's not necessary to do that to be a good correspondent. To be a really good correspondent, you've got to tell things as they are. I don't mean ridiculous efforts at fairness just for the sake of being fair—going to cover a concentration camp and finding bodies all over the place and then writing that up into your lead and in the second paragraph saying, "But Mr. Himmler said, however..." But to be a watchdog—no, I would say that's not our job.

You do the best you can until you become so involved that you no longer can regard yourself as fully objective. On my last day in Saigon [in 1975], as the helicopter was lifting me away, I was in tears. I was not being a correspondent. I had no thought of writing about it, although I knew I would eventually. I was thinking of only what was being lost and the human tragedy that was playing out on the ground. In the final weeks of the war, I devoted at least as much of my time to trying to arrange for refugees, particularly in our *New York Times* family, to get out of the country on the CIA black airlift—the clandestine airlift that took so many people to Guam. That probably occupied much more of my attention and interest and passion than filing stories for the *New York Times*, which was a remarkable failure for a journalist. I mean, that's certainly not the way you're supposed to go. But at a certain point, your profession breaks down in the face of your human feelings, and nothing can be done about that, I guess.

I came away from the Vietnam War fairly disillusioned with the possibilities of journalism in general. Most of us who were in Vietnam believe that our constituency was the American public, and that our duty was to provide as much useful material as possible to Americans in general so that they could make the right decisions. And I came to realize that, in fact, the knowledge that we were attempting to impart to our beloved countrymen was either being short-circuited or absorbed in ways that had nothing to do with the reality that we were appreciating.

It's sometimes said that the press caused the loss of Vietnam. I think people who argue that way just have no appreciation or understanding of what journalism is all about. I think that, on balance, the war would have had no other conclusion if there had been not one correspondent present. That's a terrible thing to say, because in my case, it means that I wasted about a decade of my life—except for the fact that the varieties of experience afforded by a war, in particular the one in Vietnam, were enriching. I think there's no question I came away as a better human being for having been there. But in terms of having helped America over a bad spot—I would say no. Just none of it.

War is one of the evils that beset the human race whenever people are too stupid to do the things they need to do to avoid it. And journalists—conscientious journalists, who are less interested in beating a drum for some cause than in just breaking open the facts such as they are—serve a function that's vital not only to our country, but to any country that's in a similar situation.

One of my heroes is William Howard Russell, the *Times* of London correspondent who covered the Crimean War with such dis-

He irritated Lord Raglan [commander of British forces] so
that he was forced off the military reservation near Bala-
: was denied rations and quarters; he was denied transport;
he was denied access to the telegraph. Raglan did everything he
could to have the *Times* recall William Howard Russell, and yet
Russell reported the glories of the charge of the Light Brigade and
"the thin red line tipped with steel," and most of all the cholera-
ridden hospitals and the total contempt with which the British government seemed to regard its own troops. He corrected that. He
caused the government to fall and effectively ended the Crimean
War, one of the most stupid wars the world had waged up until the
time of Vietnam.

Over the years, we've seen [the animosity between the military and
the press that began in Vietnam] cultured, fertilized, and intensified,
so that the same problems come up with no resolution in sight. A
few years after Vietnam came the great Grenada war, in which the
United States invaded this little island in the Caribbean, and after
a long and bitter battle against some very surprised Cuban advisers,
the United States won. This was a war in which the Pentagon for-
bade the presence of any news correspondents until it was all over.
This led to the conclusion on the part of many officers—and I've
spoken to some of them—that Grenada was the first war that we'd
won, unequivocally, since World War II, and it was the only war
not attended by correspondents. Therefore, a causal relationship:
Keep the correspondents out and things will go fine.

This was developed into a major thesis of policy that was full-
blown by the time the Gulf War came along in 1991, and it was
applied rigorously there. It was very easy to find miscreants crawling
over the desert and nail them with military police. Most of the real
trouble that correspondents had in the Gulf was being arrested by
MPs all the time. I think General [Norman] Schwarzkopf was sym-

pathetic to the press. At least, he seemed so. But he made it no less difficult to have access to the fighting. I was so frustrated at one point that I joined the Saudi press pool because I knew I had a better chance of getting into combat—and did.

Certainly the Gulf War, with all the constraints and controls that were placed on correspondents, served as another object lesson to the Pentagon. If you can't keep the press out, muzzle them in one way or another. Deny them access to the battlefield. Keep them away from clandestine operations, like the airfields from which the Stealth fighters operated. Do everything you can to control the situation and things will go all right for you.

I have the impression, in the case of the Gulf, that the American public was probably misinformed about the effectiveness of some of the weapons that we brought to bear, particularly Patriot missiles, for bringing down Iraqi SCUDs. I think that probably we did the Iraqi infrastructure much less damage than was claimed at the time. I also think it was unfortunate that the American public was once again steeled in the belief that as long as you keep the correspondents out, you can have a short, surgical war that will clean up all the mess. I think at this point there's practically universal support for the U.S. military among Americans, and the whole Vietnam era is completely forgotten. As we have more and more small-scale wars, the support will inevitably go to the military and not to the news people.

Despite the fact that the United States is a free country, we've never had very much regard for the press. I have the feeling that Americans, in general, tend to mistrust their news media and tend to trust people like General Schwarzkopf—the obvious hero types. Even General [George] Patton is remembered as a great American hero instead of as a kind of a fascist whose ideas of warfare were not materially different from those of his opponents in Germany. That's what we like. We like heroes. We like Special Forces. We like strong military leaders. We like winners. We don't like the wimps, who are represented by the American press corps.

FOR FURTHER READING:

Malcolm W. Browne, *The New Face of War* (Bobbs-Merrill, 1965)

———, *Muddy Boots and Red Socks: A Reporter's Life* (Times Books, 1993)

# DAVID HALBERSTAM

## VIETNAM

*David Halberstam came to be not only the most visible representative of the Young Turk reporters in Vietnam in the early 1960s, but also a symbol of a new breed of iconoclasm in American journalism generally. With his reporting for the* New York Times, *and an influential book about the Vietnam policymakers,* The Best and the Brightest, *he led his generation of reporters toward unprecedented confrontations with high authority.*

*After covering the civil rights movement for a small paper in Mississippi and the Nashville* Tennessean, *Halberstam moved to the* Times *and was sent to cover a war in the Congo, a key hot spot of the early 1960s. When Homer Bigart's six-month assignment to Vietnam was approaching an end in mid-1962, Halberstam was chosen for the Saigon post. He was a youngster replacing a legend. Yet it was a mark both of his outsized personality and of his prowess as a reporter that he soon loomed larger on the scene than Bigart had himself. Halberstam became the principal target of an effort by the Kennedy administration to discredit the young reporters by fair means or foul, and to have Halberstam himself taken off the assignment. He remained and won the Pulitzer Prize for foreign correspondence.*

———

We were young. Almost all of us were single. It was the assignment we'd all wanted. As a journalist, I've had moments a couple times in my life when I really knew that what I did mattered. I felt that way covering the civil rights movement, and I felt that way very much in Vietnam. You know you're on a cutting edge of history, that people are paying attention, that this is why you go into it in the first place. You don't go into it to be the garden correspondent, to write up a Kiwanis Club luncheon. You go into it for the chance to get that assignment.

I was twenty-eight. I'd started out on the smallest daily in Mississippi. I'd done four years on a very good paper in Nashville [*The Tennessean*]. I'd done a lot of civil rights reporting. I had always dreamed that one day I would go overseas for a great paper like the *Times* and maybe I'd be a war correspondent. And here I was, overseas for the *Times*.

It was not just covering a war, but a war that was a judgment call. Therefore, the judgment of the reporter really mattered. It wasn't just covering combat. There was a political role that was terribly important that depended on your judgment. This was everything I'd ever wanted, it was everything I'd hoped to be, and it was also something I thought I was skilled at doing. So it was a great assignment—besides which you had these great colleagues.

I was talking with my wife the other day and something about Vietnam came up, and she said something like, "That was the happiest time of your life." And I thought, "No, no, I think this is a

better time." I said it was the last moment of my boyhood, when I
had no responsibilities other than doing what I loved, something I'd
always wanted to do, something I'd trained to do. I had the friends,
the colleagues, that I'd always wanted—people like Neil [Sheehan,
of United Press International, later of the *Times*] and Horst [Faas,
an Associated Press photographer], and Peter [Arnett of the Associated Press], and people in the embassy and guys like John Vann
[a key Army source for the reporters and the subject of Sheehan's
Pulitzer Prize–winning book, *A Bright Shining Lie*]. I knew that we
were on a great story and I knew we had it nailed. So it was a great,
great feeling.

There was an embryonic sense [when I arrived in Saigon] that
the thing was not working out well, and that there would be an ever
greater division between the American Mission, military and political, and the American journalists. The American journalists whose
job it was to report on this would become the enemy. I followed
Homer, and they were seemingly glad to see me because they were
so angry at him. But I think my goodwill visa lasted about three or
four weeks, and then I think they decided I was perhaps younger
and even more obstreperous than he. You could feel the divisions
already.

When I first went there I thought we were probably on the right
side. The great, traumatic events of the Cold War had taken place
in my formative years. [Winston Churchill's] "Iron Curtain" speech
[in 1946] was when I was twelve. The coup in Czechoslovakia [in
1948] by the Communists against a democratic government was
when I was fourteen. The formative, important books were by [Ar-
thur] Koestler, [George] Orwell, Czeslaw Milosz, and the migration
of refugees in Europe was always east to west. So I thought American values, or western values, were probably more valid.

There was not a great literature on Vietnam at that time. Certainly Graham Greene's *The Quiet American* was a very, very important book to the young generation of reporters to which I

belonged. But we all had to unlearn things. You had to learn pain-
fully that the values that existed in central Europe did not exist in
a former colonial place. I think that we all had to go through a
major reconstruct.

It was a difficult, painful process, made all the worse by the fact
that we were systematically pounded by the embassy, by the ambassador, by the military, by the Kennedy administration, and by
the poet laureate of the Ford Motor Company, Mr. McNamara.
[Robert McNamara was president of Ford when Kennedy named
him secretary of defense in 1961.] And, of course, the right-wing
American press—people like Joe Alsop, and *Time* magazine. The
one organization that really wasn't tough on us was the CIA. Their
people on location were very much in accord with us, in general.

Of the things I'm very proud of, one was that I was hired to the
*New York Times* by James Reston, who was, I think, one of the great
journalists of his time. Perhaps equally important was that I replaced
Homer Bigart—the greatest reporter, I think, of two generations in
the most important assignment in the world at that time. He was a
hero to me. He was well ahead of his time, [doing] the kind of
reporting that later became fashionable in the '60s, in no small part
because of Vietnam—going against the grain. I was acutely aware
every day that he would be reading me—much more aware than,
say, of my varying editors, because I had such great respect for him.
If they'd started to win the war, I'd have gone in that direction. But
the things that made [Bigart] melancholy I picked up very quickly
as well.

By January of '63, the U.S. advisory commitment had been in
operation for about eight or ten months, and we [reporters] kept
picking up from our sources that it wasn't working. Again and again
and again, the ARVN [Army of the Republic of Vietnam] units were
signaling to the Vietcong that they were coming, so that the VC

could clear out. They would leave an escape hatch for the VC so there would be as little confrontation as possible.

We were learning from our sources—American senior advisers—that their counterparts [in ARVN] were afraid to lose troops, because if they lost troops, President Diem would regard this as a humiliation, a loss of face, and they would lose their commands. So you had this blockage. All this American energy and military skill was going to an ARVN division commander, but he wasn't acting on it. We would get this stuff again and again, wherever we went—"We get great intelligence, but they won't respond."

———

*In January 1963 there was a key test of the South Vietnamese Army's will to fight, and therefore of the basic premise of U.S. policy. U.S. advisers had been desperately hoping for an open-field engagement with Vietcong guerrillas, who normally employed devastating hit-and-run tactics instead of standing and fighting. Such an opportunity presented itself at the village of Ap Bac, close to Saigon, where a South Vietnamese division led by officers hand-picked by President Diem appeared to have trapped a much smaller Vietcong force. But the Vietnamese leaders, fearful that Diem would sack them for taking casualties, held back and watched as their force was humiliated by the Vietcong.*

———

Ap Bac was important because it was the classic moment when they had the intelligence—they had a VC battalion in the treeline—they had the helicopters, they had the technology, they had armored personnel carriers, and they deliberately let the VC get away. So it was the palpable, tangible symbol of all the stuff that had been going on. It had been going on, but it was too minuscule. You couldn't pinpoint it, you couldn't define it. There wasn't enough to hang on to for a story. But a couple of Americans were killed that day, a couple of helicopters shot down, so it encapsulated everything. It became the tip of the iceberg.

John Vann had been in-country about eight months, maybe ten months, and he was furious. He talked openly [about the battle to Neil Sheehan and me], and it just drew the line so clearly.

Classically—and this was very important—the senior American people in the Mission, rather than trying to find out what went wrong, wanted to turn on Vann and the reporters. They seriously considered court-martialing Vann for talking to us. They thereupon renewed their attempts to undercut people like Neil and me. [General Paul] Harkins [commander of U.S. forces] himself went down on location and said, famously, "We have them in a trap and we're going to spring it." And we *knew* they'd fled; they were gone. So an American four-star completely lost his credibility in front of us. There was a big map in Neil's office and we would draw little things on it, and one of them was a thing around Ap Bac that said "Harkins's Trap, semi-automatic, gas-operated, to be sprung at any time." I mean, you want to lose credibility? Lie to a bunch of very tough young reporters whose friends are being killed, who have seen guys their own age killed, who are risking their lives themselves. Go and lie to them and then try to court-martial their sources. That will draw lines in the sand.

———

*Headlines in the* Times *showed the trend of Halberstam's reporting:* "VIETNAM WAR A FRUSTRATING HUNT FOR AN ELUSIVE FOE"; "VIET-CONG MAINTAINING STRENGTH DESPITE SETBACKS."

———

After Homer left, we [in the Saigon press corps] were a very easy target because we were all so young—probably a median age of twenty-seven, twenty-eight, and none of us had yet distinguished himself. Later there would be five Pulitzer [winners]—Mal

Martha Gellhorn (second from right) and Ernest Hemingway (fifth from right) with officers of the Spanish Republican Guard, during Franco's bombardment of Madrid, 1937. "We were in it together," Gellhorn would later say of the Spanish Civil War. "We knew, we just *knew* that Spain was the place to stop fascism."

Andy Rooney (at right) with colleagues Charles Kiley (center) and Bud Hutton in England, 1943. Rooney covered the air war for the military newspaper *Stars and Stripes* and, as a member of the Writing 69th, was one of the first correspondents to accompany an Allied bombing mission during World War II.

Homer Bigart (second from right), Walter Cronkite (third from right), and other members of the Writing 69th prepare to accompany the Eighth Air Force on a high-altitude bombing run over Germany, February 1943. *New York Times* correspondent Robert Post (third from left) would be killed on the mission.

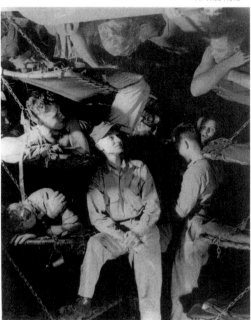

Scripps-Howard columnist Ernie Pyle, below decks on the Okinawa-bound Navy command ship *Panamint*, March 1945. Named America's "most widely-read war correspondent" by *TIME* magazine, Pyle helped to shape the national understanding of what came to be known as "the Good War."

Frank Gibney (at right) and Marguerite Higgins (third from left), with other members of the American press corps in Korea. Within two months of the outbreak of hostilities, there were more than 300 correspondents covering the story. "The rivalry was most intense," Gibney recalls, "because, in the finest tradition of American journalism, everybody congregated where they thought the story was hottest."

Correspondents accredited to the United Nations forces in Korea aboard a press train, en route to the first peace talks in Pyongyang, July 1951. Reporters covering the talks were forbidden to speak directly with negotiators or inspect documents presented at the discussions. Instead, they were briefed, for several hours each afternoon, by a U.S. Army officer who had not even been present at the negotiating session.

CBS broadcaster Edward R. Murrow (second from left) was one of the first to bring moving images of warfare into American living rooms with his 1952 television documentary, "Christmas in Korea." The production required a fifteen-man crew and a half-ton of film equipment Murrow's team dubbed "the thousand pound pencil."

Two-time Pulitzer prize–winner Homer Bigart pioneered the brand of tough, skeptical reporting that became the benchmark for the "young Turks" in Vietnam. "Being a star in those days meant that you were like Homer Bigart," David Halberstam (left) says, "that your peers thought you were best of show."

Peter Arnett (right), Malcolm Browne (left), and photographer Horst Faas in the cramped Associated Press office on Saigon's Rue Pasteur, 1963. "It was the hardest working bureau that I had ever been in," Arnett recalls, "and I'd been in this business a long time."

Mal Browne's photographs of Buddhist monk Thich Quang Duc's suicide appeared in newspapers around the world and fueled opposition to South Vietnamese President Ngo Dinh Diem. As Browne put it, "that was the beginning of the end of American support for the Diem regime."

*New York Times* correspondent David Halberstam (second from left) with Green Berets near Dak Pek, Vietnam, 1962. Halberstam repeatedly drew fire from the Kennedy administration for his confrontational—and highly influential— coverage of the U.S. advisory mission. By the summer of 1963, Pentagon officials were referring to the conflict as "Halberstam's war."

CBS *News* correspondent Morley Safer (holding microphone), northwest of Saigon, c. 1966. Safer was a key figure in what came to be known as "the Television War." His 1965 coverage of the Marine "search-and-destroy" mission at Cam Ne prompted the U.S. military to issue new rules of engagement, designed to protect South Vietnamese civilians from unnecessary harm.

Ward Just (at left) covered Vietnam for the *Washington Post* in 1966 and 1967, just as public opinion in the United States was beginning to turn against the war. "I think that people quite logically began to think to themselves, 'where is the end of this?' " Just says. "The thing that really changed the course of the war were the body bags coming back from Vietnam."

Peter Arnett in Saigon, during the 1968 Tet Offensive. "I was awakened by the sound of machine guns just outside my door," Arnett remembers, "and in fact, when I ran out into the street, the machine gun post on the street outside was firing toward the presidential palace, which was under attack by the Viet Cong. There were dead bodies of MP's lying in the street, holes in the embassy gate . . . The nerve center of the American effort, suddenly invaded."

*New York Times* correspondent Gloria Emerson in Vietnam, surrounded by the sort of children whose suffering she helped to publicize. "There were so many of them," she wrote in 1973, "working the streets, living in the markets, so small and frail that the Vietnamese called them the *bui doi*, or dust of life. It seemed inhuman to refuse them help."

Chris Hedges, who covered Operation Desert Storm for the *New York Times*, openly flouted the Pentagon's press pool restrictions. At one point, while tracking down a story without an official escort, he was detained by the U.S. military for six hours, then stripped of his credentials and forcibly returned to Dhahran.

CNN's Peter Arnett in Baghdad, 1991. Arnett was the first American television correspondent to cover a war from behind enemy lines. CNN would later be accused of "giving succor to the enemy."

Christiane Amanpour, in a freeze-frame from CNN's coverage of the 2003 war in Iraq. Thanks to the U.S. military's World War II–style press policy and the widespread use of 21st century communications technology, Operation Iraqi Freedom was arguably the most reported conflict in American history.

[Browne], me, Peter Arnett, Neil Sheehan, and Horst [Faas, who] won twice.

We were finding out stuff we didn't want to find out. We were going against our own grain. We wanted the Americans to win. One of the interesting things was our own difficult reeducation process, because we wanted it to work. And then it didn't work, so we started saying it didn't work. That's when they all started attacking us, saying, "These are the guys who want us to lose."

I think the stuff we learned there made us infinitely tougher. We had a very good press corps that worked very hard. A lot of native, raw talent got funneled into a highly disciplined toughness of mind. We learned very early on that the briefings just didn't matter, that the American briefers were vouching for information that they couldn't vouch for. They were putting their name on reports from ARVN, and as such, they had no credibility. Unless it was an un-usual event, I didn't go [to the daily briefings], and even those who went, went with their eyebrows raised.

We became the enemy [of the U.S. Mission] very quickly. I can remember, in the fall of '63, there was a battle down in the [Mekong] Delta and they weren't going to get us down there. Neil [Sheehan] and I got on the phone calling General Harkins and Ambassador Lodge, trying to figure out a way to get down there. Later that day, they had a briefing at the MACV headquarters [Military Assistance Command, Vietnam]. But it wasn't by the usual captain or major, and it wasn't in the usual room. It was in a major room and every bit of brass in the country was there. There was this briefing by a two-star [general], Dick Stilwell, the slickest briefer they had; he was the rising star. And then all the way around, lined up, were all kinds of generals and colonels. It was a clear attempt to intimidate.

Stilwell began in the most condescending way. "Before I go into this briefing, some of you young men," meaning Neil and me, "both-ered General Harkins and Ambassador Lodge today about trying to get to the battle. You're not to do that anymore. They're very busy men; they don't have time for your phone calls. You will," in effect, "take down what we tell you."

I don't like confrontational reporters. I've always stayed away from the fake tough guys—you know, the kind of television guy who shouts out questions. I don't believe in that. But I mean, my heart was pounding, and I got up and said, "Excuse me, sir, but we're not your corporals and PFCs. We're here because the *New York Times*, the United Press, the AP, and *Time* magazine sent us here. And *x* number of American helicopter pilots with gunners went into combat today, risked their lives with I don't know how many million dollars' worth of gear. It was a very big battle. The American people are entitled to know. I will keep calling you, as will Mr. Sheehan. If you want to write our publications and tell them that we are being too aggressive, and that they should replace us, you go right ahead." So that was a time when lines were really being drawn, and drawn very hard, very tough, very ugly.

——

*A key development during Halberstam's tenure was the Buddhist campaign of civil disobedience against the Diem regime. Halberstam's competitor Malcolm Browne scored a world scoop with his photograph of the monk who committed suicide by self-immolation in the street. But Halberstam covered the protests as well, showing their significance in the growing crisis of the Diem regime.*

——

I thought it was a sign that the [South Vietnamese] government was incompetent. Washington was trying to put Vietnam on the back burner, because they were interested in Europe. Kennedy had been elected by one hundred thousand votes. It's a Democratic administration. They were all too aware of what had happened in the [Joseph] McCarthy era, [the idea that President Harry Truman, a Democrat, had] "lost China." That's in their minds, so they want to keep Vietnam on the back burner. So the official line was, "President Diem is respected and is [leading] this great, growing national movement." Well, it wasn't, and we knew it wasn't. The Americans were orchestrating the optimism. Somebody once said, "The two greatest exports of Vietnam are rice and American optimism."

So when the Buddhist crisis came along, what it showed was that Diem could not respond to the people of his own country. Rather than reaching out to keep as many people in the tent as possible, as you had to do if you were in a war, he regarded this as an insult and a personal challenge to him. So it just underlined the isolation of that government and the fact that there was no national well-spring of confidence, no increasingly broad, national movement.

To communicate well, you need two people. You need someone who says it and someone to hear it. I think the reporting out there was really quite good. But the country wasn't really ready to listen yet. It was early on. The American investment wasn't that big, probably under a hundred killed. We were an advisory mission, and the essential legitimacy of the American government and the American military post–World War II and post-Korea still held. Generals told the truth. We hadn't gotten to the word "spin" yet. The idea that high American military officials would lie when other people's kids were dying—that they would put political spin above telling the truth—had not come home. It took about three or four years for it to come home.

In the middle of the Buddhist crisis, Ngo Dinh Nhu, who was Diem's brother and the leader of the secret police, decided to crack down on the Buddhists and arrest them all. Neil and I and others had great sources that the crackdown was done by Nhu's elite troops. So we wrote this, and then there's this official version, put out by the government in Washington, saying, in effect, the exact opposite. And the *Times*, unable to make a call, ran them both. Homer was back in New York, and he was furious that night, furious! He went charging up to the desk, I'm told, and said, "Don't ever do that again! You always go with your man in the field! And you got a kid out there who's doing everything right! You stick with him! The kid has not been wrong yet!"

A lot of guys from the World War II and Korean War age, for a variety of reasons, did not like the direction the reporting was taking. Either they were greater anti-Communists or they didn't like the generational divide or they didn't like younger reporters. I had a bad go-round with a guy named Dick Tregaskis, a World War II guy who was very badly wounded late in the war, and I don't think he was ever the same. He had written a book called *Guadalcanal Diary*, and he'd been a hero of mine. We'd gone off into the field; I'd taken him down to My Tho and we'd spent the day with John Vann—I turned over my great source to Dick Tregaskis—and we traveled back to Saigon. It was rather silent, and he turned to me finally and said, "If I were doing what you are doing, I'd be ashamed of myself." It was like your face was slapped.

I have this reverence toward World War II people and Korean War people. My father had been a medic in World War I, and he'd been a combat surgeon in World War II, going in at the age of forty-five years old. So we take patriotism very seriously in our family. One of the things that sustained me all the time when I was taking heat on this was that I knew that my father would have approved of what I was doing. I knew that I was the son he had raised. He had died long before then, but I knew his value system and I knew that I was okay with him.

So I had this reverence for these World War II figures, of whom Maggie Higgins [was one]. I didn't know how ideological she was. I thought good reporters just reported. Maggie didn't.

———

*Higgins went to Vietnam for the* Herald Tribune *in mid-1963. She disapproved of the reporting of Halberstam, Sheehan, Browne, and their*

*like-minded colleagues, not to mention of her old nemesis, Homer Bigart.*
*She depicted the Buddhist leaders as "riot-prone" extremists fomenting*
*"wholly irreligious excitement." She reported that the war actually was*
*going well for the United States, but that the image of Vietnam and*
*the Diem regime was being "tarnished" by "typewriter strategists" who*
*were "seldom at the scenes of battle." She was quoted in* Time *as*
*saying: "Reporters here would like to see us lose the war to prove they're*
*right."*

———

I was saddened. I mean, here's [Higgins], who'd been a great
reporter; who'd been in World War II and Korea; who'd won the
Pulitzer Prize; who, as a woman, obviously had fought battles against
male gender domination. And on that story, she was just a tourist.
She was just a terrible reporter [in Vietnam]. I don't think she was
in good shape physically. She didn't have any real sources. She was
a very avid, right-wing Pentagon mouthpiece.

Over $x$ number of months, I had done this really systematic series
of stories on the decline in the delta—the fact that the VC were
becoming ever more powerful, and the ARVN would not even come
out of their base camps. Suddenly, Maggie comes in and starts saying, "We're winning the war! We're winning the war!" My stories
are detailed, they're filled with density, I've got great sources, people
like John Vann; Colonel Daniel Boone Porter [Vann's superior];
Colonel "Coal Bin Willie" Wilson; plus all the captains and majors.
Now, my guys can't put their names in the paper, because they're
gone if they do. So I have to not use their names, and the *Times* is
beginning to ask, "Can we name your sources?" I said, "No, you
can't." Maggie's guys are all named, which is a sure sign of bullshit.

I later complained to Homer Bigart about what Maggie tried to
do. He said, "Y-y-y-young man, y-you have n-n-no right to com-
plain about Maggie. She's only a problem if she's on your own paper.
You were lucky she was on the other paper."

———

*Halberstam had a notable confrontation with Marine Major General Victor "Brute" Krulak, a friend of President Kennedy's.*

———

In those days *Time* magazine had this sort of bullshitty thing they would give to their elite subscribers, "The Inside Word," a kind of a newsletter, and it would be filled with all kinds of really good, gossipy stuff that they didn't quite have enough faith in to print in the magazine. In this newsletter, which I got a copy of, Brute Krulak told people that Maggie Higgins had seen him and she had said that Halberstam had seen a bunch of VC bodies and he burst into tears.

Today, if that story were told, I'd get a Humanitarian of the Year award. But in the politics and ethos of 1963, at the height of the Cold War, that was a sign of "This guy is a wimp." It was very damaging, utterly untrue. I mean, I was taking rather considerable risks, and I felt that was a particularly cruel cut. And it was the kind of stuff that was coming out of the Pentagon every day, an attempt to undermine you with malicious stuff.

One of the things they did to try to create this artificial optimism was to fly generals into Saigon and schedule a press conference. The guy doesn't know anything about Vietnam, but he gives a press conference saying, "We're winning the war." So, one day, there's a scene out at one of these things. I am at the airport, and Krulak is coming in, and I see him. I am burning with anger over this, because this story is an affront to my very being; I mean, it is an attempt to deny my patriotism, my professionalism, my courage, everything about me, and I go steaming over to him. It's the last thing in the world he expects. I mean, he's sitting back there in Washington, handing out crap like this the way they always do, and the last thing he expects is to have this person come at him.

Now, in myth and in movies, generals are supposed to be about six foot three and reporters are supposed to be about five foot five. I'm six foot three, and he's five foot five. And I go right into his face, and I say, "My name is David Halberstam. You have been putting out shit about me. Stop it, or I'll come and find you." And he starts stumbling. He goes, "Well, you know, it's—it's not an Ernie Pyle kind of war, is it? It's not an Ernie Pyle kind of war." He did not know what to do, because no one had ever called any of these people on it. I mean, steam still comes out of my ears.

There were people at *Time*, in particular, who, for ideological reasons, did not want negative reporting, because *Time* was then very much the voice of Christian capitalism—you know, whatever we do is right and what anybody else does, if it goes against us, is wrong.

There was this guy there, Otto Fuerbringer, who was the editor, who didn't believe that a little nation of little guys in black pajamas could stand up to the United States of America, and if we were reporting negatively, we were not made of as stern stuff as he was. So every time we would write critically, they would attack us in their "Press" column, which was then quite influential. They were going against the reporting of their own people on location—Charlie Mohr, who was writing that the war in Vietnam was being lost. *Time* got the war systematically wrong from day one.

Otto decided that he was going to win this war. [Fuerbringer visited Vietnam,] and [the U.S. military] showed him all their toys. They were building this great infrastructure at Cam Ranh Bay, and Otto looked around and he said, "I know how we can win the war in one day," and someone said, "Well, how?" And he said, "We'll bring the five top VC generals here, and we'll show them this, and they'll surrender."

You have to understand that there was a World War II generation running things, and that was very true at the *Washington Post* and a number of the magazines—people who always said, "America's going to win, and generals and high public officials tell the truth." In addition to the World War II mentality, the *Times* did not want a confrontation with the president of the United States. Having said that, in general, it behaved very well. It ran those stories. The top people there were uneasy. There's a famous story when in the fall of '63, [Arthur H.] "Punch" Sulzberger, newly minted as publisher [of the *Times*], goes for his first meeting with John Kennedy. He's going with Scottie Reston [then chief of the *Times*'s Washington bureau], and he's very nervous—president of the United States— and Scottie says, "Don't worry, he's going to ask you about your kids and you ask him about his kids. It's all very pleasant."

So he walks through the door and the first thing Kennedy says is, "What do you think about your young man in Saigon?"

[Sulzberger says,] "We like him fine."

"You don't think he's a little too close to the story, do you?"

"Oh, no, no. We think he's fine."

"You weren't thinking of moving him to Paris or London or Rome, were you?"

"No, we were not."

I mean, he held his turf. I was supposed to go on a two-week break in Hong Kong, and I got a cable saying, "Don't go on it." I think it's a great moment.

A few years ago, the *New Yorker* was going to do a photo of a bunch of us, "The Boys of Saigon"—me, Horst, Peter, Neil, Mal. We went to dinner the night before the photo, and we look over and there's Punch Sulzberger having dinner with Sydney Gruson [a longtime editor and executive at the *Times*]. We sent them a bottle of Dom Pérignon with a note saying, "We could not have done it without you." It's easy to find a reporter who'll do a good job. It's very hard to find a publisher who will stay the course. The *Times* gave me enough rope right through to the very end. That is a very nice moment in American journalism, a paper behaving with great honor in a bad moment in a bad war.

. . .

We all knew that we were rolling the dice every day. All of us thought it was an extraordinary story, that this is why you wanted to be a reporter or a photographer, and it wasn't about money. And it wasn't about being a star—not the way you're a star today. Not this goofy stuff on television, where these lightweight people make $7 and $8 million a year for being on magazines where they don't really do any reporting, where they do a shtick but they're cosmetically attractive. Being a star in those days meant being like Homer Bigart—that your peers thought you were best of show. And you wanted that. You wanted to be known as someone who was the best of the breed, and to do that, you wanted to go and do the toughest assignments. And you knew out there that this one mattered, that this was a war where what the government was saying just wasn't right. Whether we should be there or not, that's another debate. But whatever it is, as long as other people's kids are dying, your job is to tell as much truth as you can. That meant being a journalist in Vietnam had, I think, a nobility to it.

There was a dynamic that begins a little bit with Homer, much more with our group [of reporters]. There was an escalating sense that you could stand back from the assumptions and judgments of the American military mission in Saigon and Washington, that you did not have to accept their givens, that you could go out and report contradicting evidence.

Americans could sit at home and turn on the war [on television]. I think eventually it worked against the war because it caught the disproportion of it. The richest, most powerful country in the world was using its high technology in a war where that technology was not applicable, involuntarily brutalizing innocent people in this peasant country. I think what television caught was that the proportions of the war were wrong, and I think it gradually burnt out public support.

It's probably very comforting for a lot of people who were in the Quartermaster Corps and for people who never were there to feel that [the press] lost the war. What lost the war was that the policy never worked. It was part two of an ongoing anticolonial war, and the other side had a political dynamic that worked. When we talked about our Vietnamese generals, we were talking about former French corporals. And what won it was the battlefield valor of the other side—the dynamic they had, the willingness to pay an extraordinary price against the mightiest army in the history of mankind. We dropped more than twice as much tonnage in Vietnam from airplanes and ordnance as we did in all of World War II. There were no targets. The Ho Chi Minh Trail wasn't a superhighway. It was the willingness of a generation of Vietnamese who, for a variety of reasons, were willing to pay a price so that Vietnam would be Vietnamese and its future would not be determined by either the French or the Americans.

We're always a good scapegoat. Whenever you bring unconventional information, unwanted information, to ordinary people, they're not going to like it. You're an easy target when you tell people things they didn't want to know. It's very interesting. Reporters who would have been adored, like Ernie Pyle in World War II—Peter Arnett or Morley Safer or Jack Lawrence, a Vietnam version of an Ernie Pyle—were telling them things that had deep political consequences. World War II was a good war. We were on the right side. We were the armies of democracy against imperial Japan and genocidal Nazi Germany. In Vietnam it was much more complicated, because we were fighting alongside an anti-Communist Vietnamese force against what we said was Communist, but which, to the Vietnamese, looked like a nationalist force. So we made a good target.

I didn't like being called a Communist and a coward. Lyndon Johnson later called Neil Sheehan and me traitors to our country. I thought the other side was going to win, and I thought my job was,

effectively, that my readers not be surprised when the V_
into Saigon. It took a lot longer, but it happened, and I think u.
was our job. When presidents and high politicians are having press
problems—George Reedy [one of Johnson's press secretaries] is
the one who told me this—it's a sign they're having constituent
problems, because we're the early warning system. We're profes-
sionally tuned people. Homer Bigart knew where to look. I wasn't
in those days quite as quick to find the cutting edge, but I found it
very quickly, and it showed that the war wasn't being won. That's
why we jumped on Ap Bac, because it was this tangible symbol
of a failure of policy. That's your job, and you're very proud to
do it.

[The] Tet [Offensive] brought it home. Here was all this stuff coming out of the White House—"light at the end of the tunnel," "victory is around the corner," "they're gonna tumble out of the trees."
And suddenly they're at the gates of the American embassy. People
realized we had not punctured their [the Vietcong's] dynamic. The
war is costing too much. It's disproportionate. It's beginning to take
kids coming out of the middle class. It was time to go home.

Walter Cronkite is a really, truly good man, and he represented
the American center—what ordinary Americans knew and understood, and how much difficult news they could absorb at any given
time. It made him a very good communicator, because in that cen-
trist role as an anchorman, he knew how much pain they could take.
In addition, he was a World War II guy, which meant he didn't
really like what we [correspondents] were doing early on. He would
go out there early on and all his old pals in the Air Force would
show him their newest toys, and he loved it. Guys like Morley
[Safer, also of CBS News] would try to move him to the other side;
he wasn't having it.

Tet shattered him. He went out there. He was stunned by it. He
went to see Westmoreland's deputy, Creighton Abrams, who was

going to be the next commanding general. Abrams was an old pal of his from World War II and told him the truth—that it couldn't be done. Abrams was a very good guy—really knew what was going on—and that really swung Walter around. He understood that it wasn't just a bunch of kid reporters who didn't have connections, that the military, when it was being candid, talked the same way.

I think war correspondents should go out and just do what good reporters do, which is to report and listen and figure out what's at stake and to make good calls about it and listen to many voices. If your government is doing the right thing, you will enhance what the government says it's doing. And if the government, as in Vietnam, is following a misguided, bastardized policy, that will be reflected in what you discover on location, however painful that is.

The funny thing is that those of us who were the Vietnam reporters have all these pals now who are the senior generals, because whatever else, we all did it together. I mean, people like Colin Powell are people I'm greatly at ease with now.

You ought to be very, very careful about censorship. It depends on what you mean by censorship. We never triggered operations in advance or anything like that. I think under certain conditions, there's a narrow legitimacy for censorship. But if you're in a free society, and sending other people's kids into battle, their parents and their neighbors are entitled to know what the conditions of battle are.

They tried to restrict [reporters'] movements in the Gulf War. But you can't do that. It worked because the Gulf War lasted four days. It worked because they got good publicity, and they got good publicity because the American technology worked. It was a four-day war and people were happy. It was a great couple days and then it was gone.

But you can't cheat the American people. If you have an ongoing war like Vietnam, American reporters are going to get out there, and they're going to find American kids, and American kids in uniform are going to tell them the truth, and they're going to report it.

The only growth industry in America is spin. So in the Gulf War, obviously, spin was important. And it worked, but it didn't work. There's been a great controversy about the actions of General Barry McCaffrey and whether there was a day after the cease-fire when his unit assaulted retreating Iraqi tanks. Seymour Hersh has written at some length about that in the *New Yorker*. That shouldn't be a controversy. There should have been reporters there. It's a great reminder of why we have reporters.

In the Cold War, a lot of people high in the national security business thought the Russians were lucky because they didn't have a free press. I think a free press makes us better. It brings out our best. It is a monitor to behavior. It is, with luck, a bit of a conscience. War reporting is like any other reporting. It's not always perfect. We make a lot of mistakes. But when you censor stuff, you never know if you're censoring good stuff or bad stuff. If you kill an idea, if you truncate an idea, are you truncating Bill Gates or just some dumb guy around the corner? I think it's what our strength is. I think our great, great export to the rest of the world is our Bill of Rights, our First Amendment. I think this is what the rest of the world dreams of—a just society where you can debate what is the best interest of the country.

I think there was a moment of national self-doubt after Vietnam, and it was made worse by the Iran hostage crisis [in 1980–1981] and the quadrupling of oil prices and the sense that our core, blue-collar economy was in trouble. The Japanese were doing things better. There was a kind of self-doubt or malaise, and I think that in the midst of that, these little things—Grenada and Panama—made Americans feel better. I don't know that they made us stronger. I never felt America was weak. I thought Vietnam was the wrong war, the wrong time, the wrong place. I thought it was dev- astating to a lot of people. It took fifty thousand lives on our side, and probably as many as a million among the Vietnamese. Who knows the numbers? But I never thought it touched the sources of strength in America—being an open society, our great educational system, our political system, which allows us, if things aren't going well, to throw the rascals out. We are regenerative. We are resilient. It was never like the Vietnamese were going to land in Palo Alto. Nothing we had, except the wrong kind of self-image, was at stake there.

I don't think war brings out the worst in reporters. I think it may bring out the best. Larry Burrows [a leading photographer for *Life* magazine, killed in a helicopter crash in Vietnam in 1971] was a great, elegant man, a beautiful man who was much loved by his colleagues. I still mourn him. I mourn George Clay, who was an NBC guy killed in the Congo. I think war often brings out a certain nobility, a sense that things are larger than you are, and that you have responsibilities. You are watching other young men make ex- traordinary sacrifices, and you know if you're still alive it's your own good luck.

You watch the journalists, if that's what they are, in [the coverage of the Monica Lewinsky scandal] and you think, "I don't think I'm in that profession." But I think of Peter and Mal and Horst and Charlie Mohr and Mert Perry [Mohr's colleague at *Time*] almost as part of my family. Neil is like the kid brother that I never had. I remember years ago I was at some conference and Peter Arnett was talking. His bravery is so extraordinary, and I was thinking, watching him—this tough New Zealand kid who started out so rough and became this elegant reporter—and I thought, I really love Peter Arnett.

[As a war correspondent] you are witness to the most elemental thing in human life—survival, people killing people—and a great deal is at stake. You're volunteering to put yourself in harm's way. There was always a great difference, of course, between being a combat soldier and a war correspondent, because we always knew we could go home. When we got tired, when we got scared, we could go back. They couldn't.

FOR FURTHER READING:

David Halberstam, *The Making of a Quagmire* (Random House, 1965)

———, *The Best and the Brightest* (Random House, 1972)

MORLEY SAFER COLLECTION

## MORLEY SAFER

VIETNAM

*An executive at CBS News phoned Morley Safer in London at the end of 1964 and assigned him to cover Vietnam. He said Safer should stay "as long as there are stories. Three months maybe. Six at the most. American troops will be out in six months."*

*Safer, then in his early thirties, had just joined CBS. Born in Toronto, he had worked mostly for the Canadian Broadcasting Corporation, covering Europe, Africa, and the Middle East. Before leaving for Asia, he spent several weeks reading about Indochina. But as he wrote in his memoir of Vietnam,* Flashbacks, *"Nothing prepared me for what I found in Saigon."*

*Safer became best known as a longtime coeditor and correspondent of the popular CBS news program* 60 Minutes. *But he also holds a particular place in history as the television reporter most like such other*

*Young Turks as Halberstam, Browne, and Sheehan. But Safer's me-*
*dium was images, not words, at a time when broadcasting was moving*
*toward dominance over print among the news media. A single report*
*of Safer's continues to be remembered as the most powerful example of*
*how television reporting in the field affected public opinion about the*
*war.*

———

It's probably the mythology that made me want to do the work. I
was Hemingway-bit very early in my life, and that was the life I
wanted. It was the '40s version of sex, drugs, and rock 'n' roll—
seeing the world, being present at great moments. It wasn't so much
being a war correspondent as a foreign correspondent. That was
really the attraction. And of course the most exciting part of being
a foreign correspondent was covering wars.

I'd covered a number of wars before Vietnam. I hesitate to use
the word "conventional," because not much is conventional about
war. There were wars in Africa that were just scrimmages, really,
dangerous scrimmages. I had never covered Asia. I had never even
been to Asia unless you count the east side of the Suez Canal. So
it was new to me, totally. I read a great deal before I went—all the
then-classics about Indochina and the French wars. I knew a lot
about war. I knew very little about Southeast Asia and Vietnam.
And I must say, I learned a lot in a relatively short time.

———

*Safer arrived in Saigon early in 1965, just as the United States was*
*undertaking the massive escalation that would turn the conflict into a*
*full-scale American war.*

———

I witnessed the last gasp of a lovely colonial city. But what was
really quite clear to me, even after a week or ten days there, was

that something big was going on. A big war was being planned. Trees were being knocked down on either side of the main roads, and even secondary and tertiary roads were being widened for military traffic. The RMK Company was all over the country. RMK was the huge international construction firm employed by the U.S. government to put in airstrips—and not just the corrugated emergency airstrips that you can roll out on a flat patch. These were ten-thousand-foot runways for warplanes.

There was a surreal quality about what was going on, because on the one hand, you had this city of remarkably elegant people— elegant in figure and how people moved. And on the other, you had big, burly, American country boys, all looking like football players because of all the stuff they wore—the bandoliers and the helmets— big, shouldery guys on someone else's turf. You had this wonderful non-meeting of minds, which I suppose is a kind of surrealism. What added to that quality, of course, was that the war was nowhere and everywhere—no front, no place to go to find the war, [but] a zillion places to go to find the war.

[To decide what to cover] you went on instinct, partly. Partly you went on information you got from middle-level commanders, from captain to major, about operations that were planned. And even though the intelligence often was dreadful in Vietnam, it wasn't always. If they were going on "a walk in the sun," as we used to call it—on some operation, say, in the Highlands—there often was good reason for that operation, from the military point of view. I mean, intelligence was often late, or old, but sometimes it was right on the money. So that's where they wanted you to go. By "they," I mean editors everywhere. They wanted you to go over there and cover the war. They didn't want to know about the minutiae of Vietnamese politics.

I think that was a major weakness. I wouldn't say, defending my colleagues, it was a weakness of the press. It was certainly a weakness of editors and publishers, who had no interest in it. They wanted bang-bang stuff. They wanted bodies. They wanted air strikes. They wanted napalm going off. Not just television, I should add. The newsmagazines wanted it and the newspapers wanted it.

Vietnamese politics was very, very complicated. We're talking about dozens of parties, the ambitions of various generals, of the religious parties—more than just the Buddhists—of the quite genuine neutralist movement. And the tragedy, by the way, is that if that political story had been reported in a relentless way—this may just be pie in the sky—I think perhaps the war could have been concluded much earlier. Probably in the same way, but earlier.

For the most part, the military loved the press. I'm talking about 1964, '65. The relationship changed substantially over the next seven or eight years, but it was a pretty good relationship for all kinds of reasons. I had friends in the military and the military had friends in the press. A lot of officers genuinely liked journalists, genuinely wanted to tell them the truth. Some of them had an agenda. There's no question that some of them thought the war was wrong, and not a war America should be fighting. Others had an agenda, say, that the war should be fought, but not this way. And a lot of them were guys with extraordinary ambition and not much more, and [wanted] to get their faces plastered all over the newspaper and television. Plenty of that, too. But for the most part, it was a good relationship.

What a lot of the older commanders couldn't understand—and I'm talking about the level, say, from colonel up—was, "Why aren't you getting on the team?" Having a beer or dinner with some of the fairly senior commanders—"Why can't you guys get on the team?" They really didn't understand it. These were guys raised on the relationships of Ernest Hemingway and Ernie Pyle with the military, with the G.I. Joe idea of, you know, enormous sacrifice by gallant men for a worthy and important cause.

Beginning with '65, as the big U.S. buildup began and whole units came in—including whole information departments with each unit—these PIOs, public information officers, were anxious to get their

guys, their bosses, their generals on television and in the newspapers.
So they were very aggressive in trying to get us to do stories on
them. I mean the full range of stories, from civil action, providing
fresh water and medical help to villages, to actual combat operations.
And they were competing with each other. You'd get a call saying,
"Come on, how come you don't come out with the Marines? I know
you guys were out there with the First Infantry Division. Come on
up north. Come up to our place." It was that kind of silly competition. It was as keen as the competition among the reporters.

I must say, right from the beginning, that I think that the guys who
fought in Vietnam may have been the best army America ever
fielded. I think they were remarkably good and remarkably brave,
and they put up with the most miserable kind of conditions. Any
correspondent you talk to will have a dozen stories of extraordinary
bravery and acts of kindness. At the same time, they were probably
the worst-led army that any goverment could hope to launch. Officers were driven by pure and simple ambition, reveling in the war
because of its possibilities for promotion. The gulf between the guys
who were willing to fight and die and officers who were cynically
ambitious was just so obvious to me once the big war started in the
middle of 1965.

There was no censorship at all. There was restraint, certainly, and
there was an understanding that we would not report, for example,
the movement of troops until they were already in action. As far as
I know, that was never broken.

First, in order to do the job you need the people, and the military
didn't have anybody who had any training in censorship. Second,
how could they censor war news from Vietnam? Vietnam was an
independent republic—that was the myth of the time—and to impose American censorship on a war in Vietnam would have put the
lie to everything we said about helping this independent, democratic,

freedom-loving people. Then, if you had censorship in a big war like that, you would have to have censorship not only in English but in French, Italian, Russian, Yugoslavian, Spanish. I mean, it's not a simple business being a censor.

Either [the editors and producers at CBS] used the piece I sent or they didn't use it, and they pretty much used everything. There wasn't the kind of communication back and forth [that exists now]. In this day and age, correspondents have to follow their scripts. [In Vietnam] you were lucky to get a telex through, believe me. Nature and technology forced them to either accept or reject. There wasn't really a middle ground.

———

*In August 1965, Safer agreed to accompany a Marine unit on an unusual mission to a village called Cam Ne. What began with Safer's routine effort to find some news led to a historic television news report.*

———

I had a jeep in Da Nang, and the afternoon before, I went out and did a little tour of some of the Marine Corps units to find out what was happening, to see if anybody was going on operations the next day, because the operations usually began very early in the morning, four-thirty, five o'clock. I came to this unit and they said, "Yes, we're going on a search-and-destroy in the morning. You want to come along? Please come along."

We went out in a bunch of APCs [armored personnel carriers] and some amphibious vehicles, because it was down the river and then through some pretty high-water rice paddies. I talked to a captain, trying to get some idea what the operation was about. And he said, "We've had orders to take out this complex of villages called Cam Ne." I'd never heard anything like that. I'd heard of search-and-destroy operations; I'd seen places ravaged by artillery or by air strikes. But this was just a ground strike going in. He said to "take out" this complex of villages. And I thought perhaps he was exaggerating.

It was paddy land but not such high water. The troops walked abreast toward this village and started firing. They said that there was some incoming fire. I didn't witness it, but it was a fairly large front, so it could have happened down the line. There were two guys wounded in our group, both in the ass, so that meant it was "friendly fire."

They moved into the village and they systematically began torching every house—every house as far as I could see, getting people out in some cases, using flamethrowers in others. No Vietnamese speakers, by the way, were among the group with the flamethrower. The trooper with the flamethrower was ordered to zap a particular house, and our cameraman, who's Vietnamese—Ha Thuc Can, this wonderful man—put his camera down and said, "Don't do it! Don't do it!" And he walked to the house and then I went with him, and a sergeant came on up. We heard people crying.

Now, every Vietnamese house had a shelter of some kind. Often it was an underground dugout to store rice. There was a family down there, probably six people, including a practically newborn baby. They were frightened stiff. I coaxed; they didn't want to come out. Ha Thuc Can spoke softly to them, and he coaxed them out. The house was torched, as every house along the way was torched, either by flamethrowers, matches, or cigarette lighters—Zippos.

Those guys, by the way, called themselves "the Zippo Brigade" after that picture was published.

I ultimately got back to Da Nang, tried to file the story, and just managed to get the telex through. It took another day and a half or two days for the film to get back. Harry Reasoner was doing the news that night, and he read my telex.

Of course, the Marine Corps, on the basis of the reading of that telex, went into Red Alert, denying everything, saying that a couple of the houses were burned by collateral damage from artillery or something. It was just blatant bullshit, and that's an example of what really drove me crazy in Vietnam. I mean, if you're gonna lie, tell a good one. I mean, please.

Cam Ne was a shock, I think. It's hard for me to know exactly, because I was thirteen thousand miles away, with really lousy communication, so I only got the reverberation of the shock. I think [viewers] saw American troops acting in a way people had never seen American troops act before, and couldn't imagine. Those people were raised on World War II, in which virtually everything we saw was heroic. And so much of it, indeed, was. And there was plenty in Vietnam, too, that was heroic. But this conjured up not America, but some brutal power—Germany, even, in World War II. To see young G.I.s, big guys in flak jackets, lighting up thatched roofs, and women holding babies running away, wailing—this was a new sight to everyone, including the military, I suspect. Which is perhaps one reason why there was such immediate denial.

And the denials themselves were absurd. [Officials claimed] I had gone on a practice operation in a model village—a village the Marines had built to train guys how to move into a village. Or the whole thing was a kind of "Potemkin" story that I had concocted. There are still people who believe that.

I was getting the reverberations from a distance. Subsequently, I heard that President Johnson called Frank Stanton, who was then the president of CBS, and whom he knew quite well. He called Stanton the following morning, very early, and Stanton hadn't seen the broadcast the night before. As I understand it, the president said, "Frank?" "Yeah, who is this?" He said, "This is your president." "Yes, Mr. President?" "You know what you did to me last night?" "What did I do, sir?" "You shat on the American flag."

It was the end of a certain kind of innocence among the public, really. I mean, soldiers aren't innocent. For the most part, I think American armies are awfully good in the business of protecting civilians, of not going over the line. It happens, but not as policy, not as, "This is how we do things." And that's why it was so shocking, because it's not how we do things. And there we were, and seen to be doing it. So it had a really profound effect.

Of course, this wouldn't have happened in World War II, or if it had happened, it wouldn't have been photographed. Or had it been photographed, the photographs would've been censored. I think what makes the story most significant was that it was happening on television, uncensored, either in picture or commentary. There was a realization—perhaps least of all by the press, but certainly by the military and maybe by the public—that the rules have all changed. It's perhaps another reason why the military did not want people covering the Gulf War.

Still, I'm extremely uncertain about the effects of the coverage of the Vietnam War or of any war on attitudes and morale at home. I think what happened in America wasn't when the young people were resisting or demonstrating. It was '68, '69, when their parents wished they were out resisting. The thing stank. And that smell had reached into every household in America, including the hawks'. In their hearts they knew it was wrong. This war was a wrong war.

Everyone said, "How the hell did we get in there with half a million men?" [Somebody said] it started when the Vietnamese needed a truck. We sent the truck and then we had to send a driver. But the driver needs two guys to guard him, and you need two guys to fix the truck. Then, when it breaks, they need another truck. That's how you got from nobody to half a million people.

Wars are very easy to report. I'm talking about broadcasting, but [it's true] to some extent for newspapers as well. There is this extraordinary manmade spectacle for you—life, death, valor, all those wonderful things happening for you. It's like a big CinemaScope screen for you. It's easy to cover. All you have to do is a minimum of description, and only of what people aren't already seeing, and a little bit of explanation. So wars are pretty easy to cover. They are very dangerous and they're very exhausting, physically. But it doesn't take a lot of head work to cover wars.

I would be lying if I said, on some level, it isn't fun—the "band of brothers" kind of fun. I'm not going to get into a "good old days" business, but yes, there are elements of fun, elements of great humor, particularly in something as surreal as Vietnam. There are moments of exhilaration when you walk away alive and you feel good about being alive. But I found that I was building up an immunity to that exhilaration. At one point I wrote Dick Salant [president of CBS News] and said, "I gotta get out of here." It wasn't fear, it was despair. And he said, "Fine. Come out. Stay another two months and then come out." And I did. Of course, I went back three times.

There was always a moral and ethical problem [for correspondents in the field]. I don't think I passed a day in the field without it. It's something I feel to this day. At the end of the day, you're in the chopper and you're outta there, and anyone who says he didn't feel something about that is lying. There was a moral and ethical problem not just with the [American] G.I.s, but with the Vietnamese, too. I spent a lot of time with the Vietnamese troops, men living in the most miserable conditions, who may not have been paid for months, whose families were starving back home. Our military mocked the Vietnamese for desertion. Of course guys deserted. They had to look after their families. We mocked them for their desertion while we were filling the coffers of their generals.

The moment that sticks in my mind is when I was with a Vietnamese outfit. These guys were living in the worst shit you can imagine, with very little to eat, very little water, and under constant mortar attack. And a resupply chopper came in and we [correspondents] got out. And then, I confess, I cried the whole way home.

· · ·

Witnesses are notoriously bad, as any lawyer or judge will tell you. So I hesitate to say we're witnesses. But I think we're better witnesses than other civilians, and certainly better witnesses than the military. Now having said that, you must understand that a reporter, as a witness in a war, really sees only [a narrow, personal view] of the war at any given moment. I'm talking about the thick of it, when there are people dying on both sides, and you're trying to see what's happened and take a little bit of cover at the same time. Your world is very narrow—exciting, spectacular, and dangerous, but very, very narrow. To say that this incident, this firefight, is the war, is really a questionable thing.

I don't think that we should have this kind of vigilante idea of ourselves, going out and saying, "No, no, no!" I think the *effect* of good reporting is to be a watchdog.

[As a war correspondent] I tried to describe what was happening in this little moment, and as best I could, to say what it meant in some larger context. In a war like Vietnam, that was the very difficult part, because it was so scattered and it could happen anywhere. It could be anything from a car bomb down the street to an engagement of battalion-sized units out in the field. What does it mean beyond being exciting and dangerous and bang-bang? Does it have any bigger meaning than simply a moment in the war? That part can be very difficult.

I think there is probably a little bit of Ernie Pyle in virtually everyone's coverage at some point or another. But I don't think any of us, or many of us, felt the same kind of mission that Ernie Pyle felt about showing the life of the grunt—the G.I. Joe, his spirit, his stoic ability to take whatever both the enemy and the officers threw at him and still come out of it smiling. I don't think we felt a particular mission to do that. I think we felt great sympathy for the guys. But in the case of Ernie Pyle and G.I. Joe, everyone was on a team. Everyone believed in a cause, and it was a noble cause.

Revisionists have been trying for most of the last fifty years to say "Yes, but" about this, that, or the other minutiae, a part of World War II. But the fact was, it really *was* a war with a noble goal and great sense of national purpose, shared by reporters and G.I.s. It had everything that Vietnam didn't have.

"Who lost Vietnam?" One hears it continuously when you spend time with military officers of a certain age, even with younger ones, because they've been bred on the myth that the only mistake the American military made was giving such access to the press. The press lost Vietnam either because we were pinkos who approved of the regime in Hanoi and wanted America to lose and engineered our stories in that direction, or because we were out there to make reputations for ourselves, and you weren't about to make a reputation by offering positive comment on the war. Maybe there's a grain of truth in these—except for the lefty idea, which I think is absurd. I think there were serious, serious questions that all of us had about the absence of any particular goal in Vietnam, or any reason for the war. I mean, it couldn't be explained to anyone— couldn't be explained to us, couldn't be explained to the public, and certainly, least of all, couldn't be explained to the young men who were fighting the war.

Every time I approach the Pentagon about a story, this gets raised, either very directly or by implication—my coverage of Vietnam, CBS's coverage of Vietnam, the general media coverage of Vietnam. In the courses for information officers, they show Vietnam coverage and transcripts of newspapers and magazines, and the ethos is, "Never again will we give that kind of access."

Sometime in the late '70s or early '80s the military came up with new ground rules—much tougher ground rules than Vietnam, but I think any sensible person could probably live with them. Then came Grenada, and it was all out the window. The military came back to the networks and said, "Guys, our fault. We dropped the ball on this one. Don't worry." Then came Panama, which was even more stringent than Grenada, in its own way. There was a complete closedown. It was a much bigger affair than Grenada, and more important strategically. After Panama, they didn't apologize. They didn't say, "We dropped the ball." It was just: "These are special circumstances." By that time they were on a roll, and ready for the Gulf War, which was a complete and utter closedown, while giving the appearance, or attempting to give the appearance, of great candor and great access.

They give courses in the U.S. military on how to deal with the press, which is really how to muzzle the press. "Never again" is the very ethos of military information, Vietnam being the "never again." Never again will we offer everything. Never again will we even try to exercise candor in talking to reporters. What we will work hard to accomplish is to give the appearance of candor.

The most brilliant stroke ever in press/military relations, won by a knockout by the Pentagon, was Norman Schwarzkopf and the briefings in Desert Storm. What they achieved—and I think they did it unwittingly, but they achieved it—was to bypass the filtering system of editorial judgment. Through the good services of CNN, they got their guy right to the people. It made journalism redundant. Most Americans' knowledge of the Gulf War was Norman Schwarzkopf looking them in the eye, that huge mound of a man, addressing them just like that and then putting on only pictures of missiles that worked. No mistakes were broadcast. This was a coup d'etat by the Pentagon of the American press, the world press, ably assisted by CNN.

The reporters made a fuss. And I think the editors and publishers made a fuss—but not much of a fuss. This, remember, was the beginning of corporate journalism, the time of mergers and news divisions being looked at, about how much money coverage costs. So I think the proprietors were much less ballsy about it than they might have been twenty or thirty years earlier.

It was a very popular war. That's fine. But it was a popular war that we didn't cover. Or barely covered.

FOR FURTHER READING:

Morley Safer, *Flashbacks: On Returning to Vietnam* (Random House, 1990)

# ⊣ WARD JUST ⊢

## VIETNAM

*At an early age, Ward Just determined to make himself a novelist, and before long he became one—indeed, a prolific and honored novelist. Between the dream and its realization, Just was a war correspondent. "Journalism was a way station for me," he told an interviewer once. Until he was thirty, "I didn't really know anything. I hadn't gotten the measure of people. I hadn't seen what I conceived of as desperate situations. And that changed after I covered the war. I was over in Vietnam for a year and a half and came back and thought then that maybe I had enough inside my head."*

*Just is the son and grandson of newspaper publishers. (Both were in charge of the* News-Sun, *of Waukegan, Illinois.) He became a reporter, first for the family paper, then for* Newsweek, *which sent him to London and Cyprus, then for the* Washington Post, *which sent him to Vietnam in 1965. In a battle in the Central Highlands in June 1966, Just was critically injured by an exploding grenade. He refused evacuation until the wounded soldiers around him were rescued. He went home, recovered, and returned to Vietnam to finish his assignment. He decided to leave journalism in the midst of covering Richard Nixon's campaign for the presidency in 1968. His acclaimed memoir of the Vietnam War,* To What End?, *was published the same year.*

———

You have to remember that in Saigon everything took place in the heat. You begin with that. It was always so warm—morning, noon, and night—so you always walked around in these short-sleeved shirts, and we'd all go to tailors and have them make us trousers that breathed. I think those trousers cost about $2.40.

In the morning, we'd usually go to a place to have coffee and a croissant and to discuss the coming day. It was right on a very busy corner, and cars would be going by and there was a diesel smell to the air, and there you'd be, drinking the coffee, which was French-filtered, and eating the croissant, and there was this ghastly diesel odor. And of course in those days, we all smoked like crazy. (Some of us still do.) I mean, everybody was smoking about nine packs of cigarettes a day. So—the cigarette smoke, the diesel fuel, the heat. And there was another odd kind of perfume in the air. I think that must have come from the trees. You could sit at a particular place and look down the avenue, and there'd be trees on either side. You really could see the French influence. It had this wonderful colonial quality to it, and it took you a minute after you arrived to realize that now the Americans were the colonists as opposed to the French. But the French atmosphere in the architecture, the food, and the general style of the place was still very, very present. I'm talking now about 1966 and 1967. Later on, things changed, and the Americans overwhelmed everything. But while I was there, it really did have a wonderful, sleazy aura of corruption everywhere.

Anyway, you'd get up from your coffee and go over and have a couple of interviews. The war was not out of Hemingway or Orwell, not like the Spanish Civil War at all. It was out of Pinter and Beckett, because there was no narrative line, in the sense that there were no fronts to the war. The ideology was so confused, except that they were Reds and we weren't, and while that seemed to be the foundation of things, there was so much more beyond that. There was something essentially ironic, ambiguous, and paradoxical about the war in Vietnam. And there wasn't anything ironic, ambiguous, and paradoxical about the Spanish Civil War or about World War II. Korea was kind of paradoxical and ironic, and Vietnam was the endgame of that.

What made it so interesting is that you were certain you were looking at something absolutely new. You didn't know precisely what it was. It was as if you had all of a sudden discovered Picasso before anybody else, and you were still trying to sort out what you were looking at. Later on, the great art critics would come along and say, "All right, here's the Blue Period, and then we go into cubism and from cubism we go into a new kind of formality, and this is what Picasso was up to." But that was later. At the time, if you can imagine, the first time somebody looked at a Picasso, they said, "Wow!" But trying to deconstruct Picasso—what Picasso was actually up to when he was painting Madame Canals, for example— that has to come a little bit later. So in '66 and '67, in some odd way, we really agreed we were present at the creation of something. We were all sitting around trying to read the tea leaves and saying, "Where is this leading?" In 1966, it wasn't very clear. By 1967, it was a different matter. It was pretty clear where it was leading, and it was leading nowhere good. But that was later. At this very interesting time, we were really on the cusp of something, and we weren't certain what the cusp was.

. . .

I was writing for the *Washington Post,* and I knew perfectly well that I was read daily in the White House, the Pentagon, and the State Department—and by the ordinary Joe, the guy that all newspapermen called "the Kansas City milkman." It was a great writing task—to produce copy that could be absolutely understood on both levels. In other words, don't write up so high that you miss the milkman, and don't dumb it down. That's the last thing you wanted to do in the case of the war in Vietnam, so that what you were doing had no meaning for Walt Rostow [President Lyndon Johnson's national security adviser] or Robert McNamara [the secretary of defense].

What I looked upon as my great task was to describe military operations as precisely as I could, with as much appalling detail as I felt the newspaper would print. Because after a little while, it became perfectly obvious that in the Pentagon and in the White House, they were moving pins on a map. They were saying, "Now is the time for the great offensive in the Bong San plain," and they'd move a pin. Well, there was a consequence to moving the pin, and I was determined to show them what that consequence was. As a result, I did a lot of what you might call microwork as opposed to macrowork. After a while, I didn't think there was much macro—that the macro was all contained in the micro. So if you could do a thing about one platoon over two days' action, you could write that larger than itself. It became a larger thing than itself.

I had a theory for a while that, for reporters of my generation, irony was the voice of choice, and if irony wasn't there, it meant that one of two things had happened. You either had the facts wrong, or you had too few of them. So everything at the end of the day came out with sort of a turn.

Irony: What does irony do? It undermines. It's a quality in a piece of prose, particularly in a piece of journalism, that leaves you feeling uneasy. You feel undermined because it doesn't reach a conclusion or verdict. Irony sort of leaves you hanging, because Viet-

nam was this existential event, and I define existential as a thing
that's in a constant state of becoming. There were lots of little tiny
verdicts every day. But there was no big verdict.

After a while, I came to believe that was probably the wrong
tack—that as the war began to expand and as the body bags filled
up, irony was kind of a pop gun. It was not equal to the task. After
you were there for a while, you really wanted a heavier gun. And
then, it seemed to me, the last thing you wanted to do was to
undermine. You really wanted to deliver a verdict, and I'm not
talking about opinion. I'm talking about a verdict.

I've never done this, but if I went back and looked over my copy
from when I got there to when I left Vietnam in the middle of 1967,
I suspect that [my stories] got a lot harder. I don't mean tougher,
necessarily. It probably was a little tougher, but that isn't the point
I'm trying to make. The point is that the sentences began to march
in a concrete way, and I wasn't sliding off the dime so much. I really
began to banish the thought [of irony] from my copy, and tried to
write stories with a conclusion, with a period at the end of the
sentence and not a comma or a semicolon, so to speak.

During the Tet Offensive, I think, some young captain down in
the Vietnamese delta said: "We had to destroy this village in order
to save it." This is probably the only enduring sentence to come
out of the war, the one that goes in the *Bartlett's*. He seems to have
said this absolutely straightforwardly—"We had to destroy this village in order to save it." But the American reporter didn't hear it
that way. It was Peter Arnett, I believe. I think he was smart enough
to put that in the second paragraph of the piece, as opposed to the
lead. In any event, people back in the United States read that and
they said, "What is going on here?" I mean, that was the classic
ironic remark of the war.

I believed very strongly that there was a mysterious turbulence
under the skin of events, and you could never quite put your finger
on it. It had to do mainly with the opaque quality of the Vietnam-

ese—how difficult it was to understand what they thought about this war we were conducting on their soil. This was not so much a question of whether they were Reds or members of the "Free World forces," but a question of language. I always believed that when they spoke English, they would translate themselves from Vietnamese to French and then to English. French was sort of their native foreign language. And what would come out of it, often, was this wonderfully malleable, elastic tongue whose main objective was to find out what you wanted them to say, and then they'd say it. As you might imagine, you were in Never-Never Land most of the time, and that was true whether you were interviewing a village chief or the Vietnamese general in Three Corps.

One exception to this, of course, was Nguyen Cao Ky, the prime minister when I was there, who always found a way to make his meaning plain. That was because his English was very good—I believe it was his first foreign language as opposed to his second—and Ky delighted in making blunt and often outrageous remarks. But that was very much the exception to the rule.

During my period of '66 and '67, we were all trying to figure out what the war was and what it meant. We were trying to describe the elephant that was covered by the cloak. We were poking around this way and that, trying to discover the shape of events. There was always this thing in the war that you couldn't touch, and that was its essential ambiguity—this quality where the American Army would go out into the field and you didn't know who was friendly and who wasn't friendly. So you ended up fighting the whole damn country. That was complex. That was difficult to render both in film and in prose.

As the war wore on, the craziness infected everything. There were moments of high hilarity cheek by jowl to the most appalling events, most of them involving violent death of one kind or another. And yet [war correspondents] lived in this peculiar environment—you had an apartment somewhere in Saigon, or you lived at the Continental Palace or the Caravelle Hotel. The Caravelle was not the Ritz, but it was quite a nice hotel. The food was decent. You could get a martini or a glass of wine anytime you wanted. Then there was the life in the trenches, as it were. The two lives were extremely difficult to balance successfully.

Strangely, I think probably the last war that was anything like that was the Spanish Civil War, where everybody was living in Madrid and taking a taxi to the front. The difference in Spain was that you were under constant attack from the other side—bombs and so forth. That was not the situation in Saigon. The correspondents were sharing the danger only when they were in the field. In Saigon, you might as well have been living in—up to a point, anyway—Chicago. It was not dangerous at all. And then you'd get an airplane and go out to the field.

At the end of the day, at five o'clock, the military briefers would get up with their charts and their bar graphs and they'd tell us what went on in the war for the last twenty-four hours. They had this virtue—the descriptions were very clear, so clear that you knew they couldn't possibly be accurate. But if it was a slow day, and you wanted to hold on to the franchise for a while, you'd actually write a story out of the news briefings. Then you'd file it to your newspaper and it would lead the paper. On a slow news day in the United States, newspaper after newspaper would run this damn story you had written and the lead would be something like, "In fourteen separate actions in South Vietnam yesterday, two American advisers were killed and an estimated 150 Vietcong guerrillas wounded." It was fantasy land. It didn't bear much relation to the truth. But there it was. It was official because you put a name behind it: "Lieutenant Colonel Smith said..." That was the Five O'Clock Follies.

There was a search that went on daily. It was essentially for the wire services to find something fresh to put in the lead. And they would reach far. They reached and reached and reached. It became known as the Left-Handed Battalion Commander Syndrome, the idea being that they would find out from some briefer that, for the first time in the war, a battalion was led into battle by a left-handed lieutenant colonel.

McNamara and his computers and the people around him thought they could reduce the war to numbers, hence the emphasis on precise numbers of killed, wounded, missing. They were extremely interested in being precise about the number of enemy killed. I believe it was Frances FitzGerald who went back over a lot of the numbers over a lot of years and discovered that the number of enemy dead in any given week never ended in the figure 0 or 5. Never 65 people killed—64. Never 60 but 59 or 69 or 71. They'd go up or down just because they wanted to be seen to be precise, because that's what McNamara loved so. He just loved his numbers.

At the level of colonel on down, I think the American Army was pretty well led. The strategy was terribly flawed. I have not been able to sort out the responsibility for that strategy, whether that was a Pentagon or Joint Chiefs of Staff strategy or a civilian strategy—meaning McNamara and his people—or how much it emanated from the White House and National Security Council. General Westmoreland certainly was the one charged with carrying off the policy of attrition and he certainly seemed to believe in it. It was doomed almost from the beginning, and, oddly, Westmoreland knew that himself. When you would go out with him to the field, he'd look at some action and it would show some appalling risk that a North Vietnamese or Vietcong unit had run, and he'd shake his head and say, "They have no regard for human life." If that was true, if he truly believed that, it meant that they would fight to the last man, and there were a lot more men up in the north. That meant a policy of attrition couldn't possibly work unless you were prepared to lose, say, a half a million or a million Americans. Everybody knew that was never in the cards.

There was another quality about Westmoreland, though. He was a gent. You could not like his strategy. You could not like the way he was pursuing the war. But it was very difficult not to like him.

What's absolutely true is that none of us spent enough time looking at the overall strategy. That required you to have part of your mind in Washington and part of your mind in Vietnam. There were a few people who were able to do it, but it was not a common thing.

You could write stories without going to the front. The trouble is, they wouldn't be very good stories. It was a war, after all, and you belonged at the front no less than war correspondents of earlier generations. You had to see how the thing was done. You couldn't get that out of the five o'clock briefing. The five o'clock briefing could give you numbers. It couldn't show you the way the battle actually went. And if you saw enough of these small actions, then you could add up in your mind the actual way in which the war was being conducted—how the captains were doing it and how the lieutenant colonels were doing it and what had happened at the end of the day, when you looked at this plot of land and added up our dead and their dead—what did that mean? You couldn't do that without being there.

The American Army did everything in their power to get you anywhere you wanted to go. Typically, you'd arrive on the flight line at six o'clock in the morning at Tan Son Nhut Air Base having heard of a firefight somewhere, and you'd walk up and down the line until you found a Caribou or a Buffalo or a helicopter or a C-130 that was going in that direction. You'd say, "Can we climb aboard?" and the skipper would say, "Of course. Get on. You want some coffee?" And you'd end up in Pleiku or Can Tho or wherever the action was. They'd take you where you wanted to go, drop you off, and bring you back, and they did this with the utmost good cheer, even in the later days of the war.

I was with a reconnaissance platoon, forty people, deep in the highlands of South Vietnam. We ran into a lot of enemy soldiers. They thought it was somewhere between a battalion and a regiment of enemy. And I think within the space of an hour we had twelve dead and over twenty wounded in this group. We were bunched in very close, with the enemy all around us. Artillery fire was coming in that, in effect, saved our lives; otherwise we would have been overrun in a minute. These were very tough characters I was with, but there were literally hundreds of them, and there were forty of us.

You find yourself in an ethical dilemma, to the extent that you can think about anything with shot and shell flying around. You really don't want to do anything to make their mission any more difficult than it already is. You're nonessential cargo. You can talk about the public's right to know and the First Amendment all you want, but this is serious business. People are dying in front of your eyes. At a fairly high level, you want to stay alive yourself, but you don't want to do anything to get anybody killed. Particularly, you don't want to do anything stupid.

So, in my own case, a captain said to me, "You're gonna need this," and he gave me this .45-caliber pistol. Well, I'm a hunter. I used to hunt as a child with my father. I'd known about weapons. I didn't know anything about a .45. And the idea of all of a sudden picking up this thing—it's a huge gun, you know—and lying on the floor of the forest, waiting for some helmeted head to come up five or six feet away from me—I wanted to disappear. Because I knew that in terms of the Army, I was combat-ineffective. I hadn't been trained to do anything like this. But I was goddamned if I was going to get in their way, either, meaning the Americans. So, thank God, no head appeared, so I didn't have to shoot him, or try to shoot him. And in due course, we were rescued by the medivacs [evacuation helicopters].

I've thought a lot about that. It's essential for things of that kind to be described for people at home, and to be described as thoroughly and completely as you can do it. They have a right to know that. But if I hadn't been along, would there have been another infantryman along? And if there had been another infantryman along, maybe things wouldn't have gone quite so badly—although I doubt it, to tell you the truth. But as a supernumerary on one of these missions, you really can't help but wonder if your presence somehow changes the action, and not in a favorable way, sort of like the Heisenberg principle. Yet it must be done. It can't not be done. So you go ahead and do it, and then sometimes you think about it a little bit afterward.

The war was lost because the enemy was stronger than we were, and they would have fought for a thousand years. We could have put a million men in the country and they still would have been fighting. And they would be fighting to this day, if it took that. We did not understand the nature of the enemy. The Army, specifically, did not understand the nature of the enemy, how tenacious and tough those Stalinists in Hanoi really were. There was nothing to be done. I suppose you could argue that nuclear weapons might have helped—that is, if you simply leveled the country. "They made a desert and called it peace." Short of nuclear weapons, the war was not winnable.

After about 1966, no correspondent was reporting that things were going well and that victory was around the corner—because things weren't going well. Victory wasn't around the corner.

It's always been a little curious to me. I don't know what they wanted the correspondents to do. Actually, I do know, because in 1967, Joseph Alsop told me. He said, "You know, if you would write in the *Washington Post* that the war was won, maybe then we could get out." Joe, at that point, was very much a hawk, had been a hawk all the way along. But Joseph Alsop was no dummy, and he saw, too, that things were unraveling. His concern was honor, the honor of the nation, a pretty reasonable concern. He had an idea that somebody like me—not known either as a hawk or a dove, but writing for a very important newspaper—should say in my farewell piece that things were going much better than anyone anticipated and we could hand this war over to the South Vietnamese and let them deal with it. I listened to this one night at dinner, with bottle after bottle of Bordeaux. With a kind of a horror, I said, "Joe, write me the lead for this, please. Would you please write me a twenty-six-word lead that will encompass this thought?" So I didn't do it, and instead my farewell piece said in the headline and in the first sentence, "This war's unwinnable."

I came back to the United States in the middle of 1966, and for the first time paid real attention to the evening news. I spent some time watching these correspondents, who were now friends of mine, report some really horrendous battlefield stuff. And what astonished me was how on the evening news it wasn't real. I mean, the blood didn't look like blood. I knew by then what blood looked like, and the blood that you saw on NBC was not the way it looked in the field. None of the film could capture the enormous tension and weight of a battle—the way the people looked, the way the soldiers moved. This had nothing to do with the skill of the correspondent or the skill of the cameraman. It had to do with the limitations of film. And I thought to myself that a skilled writer can probably get closer to the bottom reality of a seriously violent action than a motion-picture camera.

January 30, 1968. I was back from Vietnam, sitting in the newsroom of the *Washington Post*. Murray Marder and Chalmers Roberts, the two national security correspondents for the newspaper, said, "We've got an interview with Walt Rostow this afternoon. He's going to give us some captured enemy documents that are going to prove the war is being won. And you're just back from there, so come along with us, and you'll have a question or two for him." I said, "Fine," so we wandered over to the White House.

We got into Rostow's office, which was this sort of little shell of an office, not a very serious office. When Henry Kissinger took over a year later, the place looked like the Taj Mahal, but it didn't then. Rostow had his documents in triplicate, and he was passing them over the table to us, and Chal was asking him, "What is this document?" and "What is that document?" And meanwhile, right over Rostow's left shoulder there was a little hole in the wall, and from time to time, a hand reached through and dropped a note on Rostow's desk. He would pick it up, look at it, put it down, and continue talking.

Finally Chalmers Roberts said, "Walt, what are these notes that you're being handed?"

And Rostow said, "Well, you boys will probably be wanting to get back to your office."

Chal said, "Why is that?"

And Rostow said, "Well, there seems to be some kind of general military action in South Vietnam. They're calling it the Tet Offensive. Our embassy has been occupied. There are people on the third floor and it's a pitched battle in the embassy." [*Rostow was repeating the earliest reports. In fact, the insurgents penetrated the grounds of the U.S. embassy but not the building itself.*]

Roberts and Marder and I were on our feet saying, "Good-bye, Walt." We're heading back to the office to find out what's going on, and the last words were Walt Rostow saying, "Boys, boys! Don't forget your documents!"

[The North Vietnamese and Vietcong] certainly lost an awful lot of people [in the Tet Offensive], and their army was combat-ineffective for a couple of years. The tremendous effect of Tet, I believe, was the utter failure of American intelligence to predict it.

One remembers now that they struck virtually every provincial capital in the country, including Saigon; hit virtually every American base and virtually every South Vietnamese base at the same time. That kind of movement of troops, in a country under surveillance, theoretically, by both the Americans and the South Vietnamese—how could this have happened unless we simply did not know where they were?

I wrote a news analysis at the time that was roundly denounced as being left-leaning or something like that—"defeatist," I think, was the word they used. To me, after Tet, the key finally turned in the lock. It was all an endgame after that. It did not seem to me to be possible that the Americans could recover. Our Army was not quite combat-ineffective, but the drug problem had grown. The number of dead each week, even preceding Tet, was at a level that the American people would simply not support. Given this tremendous intelligence failure—and what is war, after all, but an intelligence game, along with the artillery and the infantry in the field?—I didn't see how we could recover from that, no matter how badly the enemy forces were hit.

It ought to be said that more than a few of our own also died in this action, particularly the Marines up in Hue in the twenty-one-day battle for the Citadel. So this was not done cheaply. This was not the Gulf War, where they were sending in a few B-52s, and we were taking two or three casualties a day. A lot of Americans were dying. And I have to say, your heart went out to the American commanders faced with this thing that had not been anticipated. They were trying to assemble some kind of rationale for it, and the truth of the matter was that all of a sudden, things were unmasked. We weren't groping around anymore, trying to find the shape of the elephant. The cover flew off and you could see what the thing was and how dominant the Communist forces were in South Vietnam. That had not been seen before to that degree.

What effect [Walter Cronkite's commentary on the Tet Offensive] had on the American public, who knows? On the journalists, probably very little; he didn't say anything that wasn't known already. On Lyndon Johnson, quite a lot, because Johnson looked at Walter's report and said, "If I've lost Cronkite, I've lost the country." Lyndon Johnson was no fool, politically, and I think that was probably absolutely accurate—that Cronkite expressed what most Americans felt. But he expressed it better, and he expressed it in that avuncular way. No correspondent since, newspaper or TV, has had the authority and the trustworthiness of Walter Cronkite. Those words coming out of Walter Cronkite's mouth made a big difference. But the big difference was not in the public. It was in the White House, in the person of Lyndon Johnson, I think.

You have to go back to that time. In the 1960s, the press, if anything, was even more conservative than it is today—conservative in the sense of ethically conservative, personally conservative. For Walter Cronkite to speak out in the way that he did was an act of courage. He'd spent all these years building up his reputation, and a deserved reputation—a very solid, familiar character, someone who could be trusted. And then, all of a sudden, he comes back from South Vietnam and he says, "Things are not going well and here's why." It would have been easy for him to say that to a few friends around a drink at the end of the day—to decide not to go public with it because it was an editorial comment on the most divisive issue in American life with the possible exception of race. It's hard to imagine today just how divided things were. It was much, much easier for a journalist to say, "Let that cup pass from me." Cronkite decided not to do it. He put his authority on the line, something that nobody likes to do. Politicians don't like to do it. Journalists don't like to do it. Cronkite did it. You know, hats off to him.

You can hardly put the words "war correspondent" together without the image of the Camels in the pocket, the flask in the back, and the campaign hat pulled down like that. And there's just enough truth to the cliché to make it enduring. If there was no truth in it, it would have collapsed of its own weight. It really is a kind of a swashbuckling life. "High-stress atmospheres," somebody once called it. So there's something to that myth, I guess.

It's a hell of a lot more fun than covering an American political campaign, I'll tell you that. I did both. You're in a foreign country. It's usually exotic. The stories are natural. You have to have a taste for descriptive prose. The material is fabulous. I mean, the material's right in front of your eyes. So if you have a taste for it, and you do it well, you tend to keep on doing it.

When I was in Vietnam, I felt it was very important to describe things as accurately as I could for the folks running things at the Pentagon, along with the ordinary reader. I never looked at myself as a megaphone for the folks back in America. That's highfalutin'. But you do feel a responsibility to do the best that you can do. You try not to shirk. You try not to lay off. You try to be faithful to the material. That's really all that you can be—faithful to the material.

As long as there are wars, it is very important to know, in the details, how they are being fought. It's important to know the manner in which people are dying, whether it's some warlord in Africa or Bosnia or Iraq. If someone isn't there to report it, it's just a tree crashing in the forest with nobody to hear it. And it's important that people hear it. It's important that people pay attention, and sometimes you have to force them to pay attention. The alternative is there's all this random bloodshed, violent bloodshed, and nobody knows anything about it, and nobody knows who is responsible. And the journalist, the foreign correspondent, the war correspondent, has some role to play in fixing responsibility.

FOR FURTHER READING:

Ward Just, *To What End? Report from Vietnam* (Houghton Mifflin, 1968)

# ┤ GLORIA EMERSON ├

## VIETNAM

*In the 1960s, Gloria Emerson was a fashion reporter for the* New York Times. *She wanted to be a foreign correspondent and especially to cover the war in Vietnam. Though she won assignments to Northern Ireland and Nigeria, editors at the* Times *withheld the Vietnam assignment until 1970. "They finally sent me because they'd run out of men," she once said.*

*She covered the war from 1970 to 1972. Her stories reflected her own searing sense of the waste on all sides and the utter loss of illusions among those who observed the war in its last years. After returning to the United States, Emerson interviewed people throughout the country about the effects of Vietnam on their lives. The result was* Winners and Losers: Battles, Retreats, Gains, Losses, and Ruins from a Long War, *which is widely regarded as one of a small number of great books about Vietnam. Harrison Salisbury said it was "sheer agony to read…and before you are through you know that Vietnam will never be over for this generation of Americans." Emerson's reports for the* Times *won the George Polk Award for excellence in foreign corre-spondence, and* Winners and Losers *won the National Book Award for nonfiction. But Emerson says here that her "little prizes" only made her feel that "I hadn't been good enough."*

———

I had been in Saigon many years before, when the French were just leaving. It was a calm, very French city. Now [in 1970], it was a nightmare. It was chaotic, berserk. Soldiers were not allowed to come into Saigon in 1970 and '71, because they had been a tiny bit unruly. See, just the Special Forces officers came, and they were worse than anything. I was called on two occasions to go to the bar across the street to calm them down—as though, you know, I were a kind of Mary Poppins, and the sight of me would restore them to their normal sanity. They were making a mess, breaking things, grabbing girls.

Alvin Schuster was my bureau chief, and he often said he was sure I would give him his first heart attack before he was forty. Here is an example of what he meant. We were crossing the street to go back to the hotel, and I saw a G.I. being very rough with a small Vietnamese woman and trying to take money out of her purse. So I socked him in the arm and said, "Stop that, that's no way to treat a lady." And he looked at me, astonished to see me, and said, "That's no lady, it's a man." He had paid her in advance for intercourse and then discovered she was not a lady, she was an elderly boy. That kind of confusion existed on so many levels. And it was sad, with children in the streets.

I was surprised by the enormity of the Americans. They looked like young elephants. Their bones were massive, and there were so many little hideous places on what had been the Rue Catinat—Big

Boy Hamburgers—and the war had cut down the trees to widen the streets for military traffic, and that was so sad and so painful. The city had been deformed in a hundred different ways. It had a kind of sepsis. The war had gone into every corner of every life, and the Vietnamese value harmony very much. There was no harmony, there was no order, there was no calm. There was corruption at every possible level, and people were sad and nervous.

I pretty much stayed apart from the press corps. I don't drink Jack Daniel's and I didn't take dope or stronger stuff, so I stayed by myself, a little island. I needed more sleep. I had to get up and get helicopters at five in the morning. There were no serious discussions of where this was headed. It was so absurd, it was such a colossal fraud, that any serious conversation would disintegrate immediately.

I could not abide [high U.S. military officials]. I saw them as very dangerous, treacherous people who would lie at the drop of a hat. And they weren't so crazy to see me either. They didn't like women floating around. They were collaborators in the fraud, the military. They gave the false body counts—although they may not have wanted to—they told the lies, they were not independent agents. There were one or two officers who might have been marvelous, but it was not my good luck to know them.

Vietnam is a very small, narrow country, and the military was packed in and the press corps was huge and we were packed in with them. We were not censored. Of course, you were called in and reproached if your coverage was deemed slightly too negative, but reproached in the most sort of nonchalant way. You were urged to see the brighter side of things. And of course there wasn't any brighter side of things.

The Five O'Clock Follies? Oh, it was ludicrous. It was painful to see. Some briefer, a colonel, would get up there and you'd watch his trial by fire as reporters would taunt him. He was hardly responsible for the mess, but they gave such duplicitous information and figures, and after a while it was just part of the heavy sadness of it all. It was impossible even to laugh at them and their loony tunes.

I wrote a story about buying heroin among American troops and that seemed a fairly important story. I went out and bought some heroin myself, outside a military installation, and brought it back to my office. You could buy anything in South Vietnam—any pill, anything. There was heroin being sold for a carton of Salems. The drug use, when I was there, had escalated severely. People smoked heroin because, as they said to me, "Grass is loud, man," meaning marijuana smells, but heroin doesn't smell when you smoke it.

[For a reporter to hitch a ride on a helicopter] you had to check in with the military and then get someplace, but getting out you could just hop on. We used helicopters like taxis, and there was an element of shame when you were with soldiers, because they were stuck there and you felt ashamed that you could just call your little taxi and get out. I felt very bad that they were deprived of this.

[Once I told a helicopter pilot] "I'd like to go, please," and he said no. And then his copilot told me it was a hot LZ—a hot landing zone. Maybe they thought I'd bring them bad luck, but they wouldn't let me on, and I was secretly so pleased. I made a fuss, saying I must go, but I was so glad not to have to go. I didn't argue that much.

I was deeply moved by so many American troops because I knew full well that these were the working-class kids of America, and they didn't really know what was going on—that they were there to defend the government of Nguyen Van Thieu, which was corrupt, despicable, and thoroughly distasteful. They had no idea of the political significance of their being there. I think they all thought we had gone to South Vietnam in a liberal, kind way to help these people have a democracy. I did not try to educate them. I told one group of soldiers once about the World War I poets and Wilfred Owen's wonderful poem: "My friend, you would not tell with such high zest, to children ardent for some desperate glory, the old lie,

*Dulce et decorum est pro patria mori.*" I had to explain the Latin: "'Tis sweet and fitting to die for one's country." But they loved it. And I said, "That's the old lie, isn't it?" And they understood very well. But I didn't do that often because we were busy and they were busy being soldiers.

There wasn't a mutinous spirit [among the soldiers I met], but there was a kind of insubordination floating around. I thought it was quite wonderful, a great sign of health, and they wore the oddest jewelry. They looked like the cast of *Hair*. They took their boot laces, which were black, and made bracelets and necklaces and wore peace signs and FTA ["Fuck the Army"] on their helmet covers. It was not a sight to lift the heart of any man who went to West Point. But I thought it a sign of health. They so resented being there. They knew at this point, by 1970, they were being used badly.

[Contrary to the view that television brought war's brutality into American homes] what you saw on television was really quite pure, and not the nasty things that we all saw. They weren't allowed to show the badly wounded. Nobody ever died on camera. You never saw any boy with his intestines coming out. It was sanitized, and it had to be. You never saw an American corpse on television. You saw fighting. But the living room war is a curious mistake.

There were brilliant television reporters like Jack Lawrence, this mournful, small figure would make a commentary and your heart would shrivel. There was Morley [Safer]. And there were photographs. The photographers were the great stars of the press corps.

The massacre [of scores of civilians by U.S. soldiers at the hamlet of My Lai] was March 18, 1968, and [Seymour Hersh's] story ran the following year on November 13. Many people denied it, didn't believe it, even though there were photographs. Isn't it peculiar that with this huge press corps in South Vietnam, Americans and foreign, the most important story of the war came out of America, and was written by Sy Hersh, who had not been to Vietnam but who tracked down Lieutenant [William] Calley [who ordered the massacre] and found him in Fort Bragg? It tells you what a great reporter can do outside the war zone. Maybe you don't have to go to a war to do the best reporting on it.

No reporters were taken on that operation, and if you weren't taken on an operation, you'd have to get the story from one of the soldiers who had been there, but they weren't talking. We didn't even know about the operation. We didn't know about dozens of military operations that were going on. What it really means is that Sy was smarter and more persistent and more driven than anyone else.

Maybe it was because I was older than the average correspondent— I was already in my thirties, well into my thirties—but I started noticing how many of [the soldiers] had cowlicks, how young they were. When they went into combat and came out, they weren't young anymore. We all knew that. But just coming into the field, they looked like a high-school class, and sometimes when I was with a badly wounded boy, I would think, does his mother know, wherever she is, that her son has been so hurt? Will she get a strange feeling, in the kitchen or driving a car, that her child has been grievously injured? That used to upset me terribly.

Of course, the American troops were young and big and healthy, but sometimes you saw a boy who didn't look so peachy, and it turned out that often enough he was a victim of [U.S. Defense Secretary] Robert McNamara's Hundred Thousand project. I should say that I have a consuming hatred for Robert McNamara, and long to be in a room alone with him with a kitchen knife in my hand. Robert McNamara devised Project One Hundred Thousand in the mid-'60s to lower the qualifying physical and mental exams for the Army. And by doing so, he got kids who weren't quite able to get through the war. A doctor once showed me a boy who as a child had had rheumatic fever, which is an inflammation of the heart and joints. He had been drafted. They were so hungry for young bodies, preferably from the working class, not from Harvard or Dartmouth. Then I saw a boy who had had a farm accident; the tip of his rifle finger, the right index finger, had been chopped off when he was a kid. He was in the Army. And I thought Project Hundred Thousand was the most despicable plan and that Robert McNamara should have been criminally prosecuted. But alas, that did not take place.

[Some in the military blame the press for the defeat in Vietnam.] What else are they going to say? We lied? We failed? We did not comprehend? There's a famous story that Bob Simon of CBS tells, that when he was in Desert Storm an officer who remembered him from Vietnam went up to him and said, "Hello, Bob, come back to lose this one for us, too?"

The press wasn't that good. There were many great reporters, and people tend to think of the whole press corps as those great reporters. But there were hundreds of people who were toeing the line. I don't think the average civilian thinks the press lost the war. But in a survey of officers of field-grade rank, they blamed it on television, because they're incapable of going beyond the first bare outline of an idea and analyzing the war. Well, I've never been a general, so maybe there are problems I don't fully understand.

The hardest thing is afterward, when you're not so busy and the memories come back and you try to understand the memories but it's impossible. It was so horrifying and so useless and so wrong. Martha Gellhorn used to call it a war of crime. She said that to me. It was such a waste of lives—the Vietnamese and the Americans and the Cambodians and the Laotians—that there's no way you can take a deep breath and smile and say, "I did well." If anything, the little prizes haunt you. I once walked by a bookstore in Beverly Hills, on Rodeo Drive or some fancy place, and saw my book in the window, *Winners and Losers,* and I was so ashamed that I hadn't written a better book that I went inside and put it down so people wouldn't see it. I had the most piercing moment of shame that I had taken this catastrophe and dared to put it in a book.

I don't think any one of my stories made a difference. If they did at the time, that was fine, but they were like ice cubes. They melted in the sun. The people whose work didn't melt were the photographers. They have left a stunning reminder of their achievements. Many of them are dead, of course. You can't look at the work of Larry Burrows [of *Life* magazine] and Henry Huet and not see the brilliance and the tenderness and the blackness of it. Nobody remembers a story that was filed for a newspaper, but people remember photographs. Henry Huet took a photograph of a wounded medic cradling another wounded soldier in his arm, and trying to feed him from a C-ration can, and at one point he takes a napkin to pat the man's mouth. I couldn't look at that photograph without weeping at the sight of so much love. It was the contrast between the love and the murdering that was very difficult to embrace.

We were surrounded by civilians who were suffering. You couldn't walk three blocks in Da Nang or Saigon or Qui Nhon without seeing it. Remember, we did have an American program called Brighter Life for War Victims, and I once asked an officer in the Brighter Life for War Victims program if perhaps we shouldn't leave, and then they'd have a brighter life. But he found it very difficult to grasp what I was saying. He wasn't accustomed to my sarcasm.

When you write about pain and loss, you have to be very strict with yourself and not indulge your own emotions. It can't be too sentimental. Be honest and report what the person is feeling—the loss of a pig, the loss of a leg, the houses burned down by Americans. All that can be scrupulously reported.

I thought Christiane Amanpour did it brilliantly in Sarajevo, in that very rapid, stuttering, English voice. They buried a two-year-

old girl, but so many people had been killed in the shelling that
they didn't have enough numbers to put on her gravestone for the
year she died, so they had to leave off the last one. Her age was
two and a half. Christiane did a beautiful broadcast about that. So
many dead they ran out of numbers.

Christiane told me about the camerawoman who worked with
her in Sarajevo who had been shot in the jaw and chin by a sniper,
which means he was able to pick his target very precisely and knew
what he was doing, and it was so appalling that she said when she
had finished working and was walking in the streets of Sarajevo, she
made this futile but hopeful gesture of holding her hands up to her
face, so that she couldn't be disfigured.

Not every reporter lifted their hand and stepped forward to go to
Vietnam. But it's hard for men to say I can't, I won't, I don't want
to, because they don't want to be thought of as cowards. Is that not
so? Not everyone grows up wanting to be a war correspondent. But
an awful lot do. It's a good story. It's a running good story full of
color and drama and danger, and that's very popular with young
men. Is it not? Men think it's very dashing—some old movie with
Joel McCrea, you know, the trench coat, the legendary feats, the
praise. How else can you go to war and not be a soldier? And I
think people like going to war. And if they go as a war correspondent they're in less danger than the soldier and they don't have to
do the killing.

[The war correspondent's proper role is] to make clear what is
happening in the country where the war is taking place and the
effects of the war and why the war. To tell the truth, if he can or
if she can, not to buy the party line. To resist all propaganda em-
anating from your own government and the officers in your own
army. Standing strong and finding out as much as you can for yourself.

Every shot soldier is a story from the Spanish Civil War on up to Vietnam, and perhaps in Iraq. You have to be very careful not to be too sentimental. You have to write with a bit of dry ice.

For a long time the *New York Times* would not run a picture of a napalm victim on the grounds that that was too horrible. And then they did. I think it should be reported, every detail should be reported. We should know everything that happened at Srebrenica, we should know everything that happened at Kosovo, and then we should be educated in how to prevent our country from going to war. That is our highest calling.

I think it was David Halberstam who wrote somewhere that Vietnam was the sorriest story ever told and he wished we could have all done better. For many years, as my little prizes drifted in and people stopped me on the street, I knew I hadn't been good enough, that I should have taken even more risks, that I should have tried even harder. It simply demanded more than my resources permitted. I did not soar to the heights that I had every reason to expect I might. It weighed too much, I couldn't carry it, I couldn't go any further than I did. And that's very sad, isn't it—to have to live with that and be praised all the time? It makes one feel like a fraud.

One great story comes in your life and holds you forever. In my case it was Vietnam.

I wish I'd had Spain instead of Vietnam. I wish I'd had something to say yes to. I can't imagine what a privilege that would be. I'm for that—"I'm standing behind this army." But it didn't happen, did it? Nothing to say yes to.

FOR FURTHER READING:

Gloria Emerson, *Winners and Losers: Battles, Retreats, Gains, Losses, and Ruins from a Long War* (Random House, 1976)

# —=| PETER ARNETT |=—

## VIETNAM · PERSIAN GULF
## AFGHANISTAN · IRAQ

*In Vietnam, Peter Arnett was a reporter's reporter, winning a Pulitzer Prize and staying with the conflict until the end. He was revered within his profession but not much known beyond it. During the Persian Gulf War in 1991, his relative obscurity ended. Working for the fledgling Cable News Network, he became CNN's representative—and the only western reporter—in Baghdad for most of the war. His coverage from behind enemy lines, under Iraqi censorship, became controversial in the United States. As Arnett explains here, he covered the Gulf War from Baghdad to be true to the mission of CNN, which was determined to be a truly international network. For ten days he worked alone, sending reports from a suitcase-sized satellite telephone as nervous Iraqi officials stood at his side. The censors, as it turned out, were hardly zealous Baathists, and Arnett was able to report the war from the receiving end of American power—a perspective the U.S. public had seldom, if ever, seen before.*

*In 2003, Arnett returned to Baghdad to cover the U.S.-British war to oust the regime of Saddam Hussein. This time he was working for the MSNBC program* National Geographic Explorer *and NBC News. He reported the "shock and awe" bombing of Baghdad and the air strikes that followed—the coalition's attempt to win the war with a quick "decapitation." Ten days later, when the U.S. ground advance had slowed, Arnett granted an impromptu interview to Iraqi state television. He said: "America is reappraising the battlefield, delaying the war, maybe a week, and rewriting the war plan. The first plan has failed because of Iraqi resistance. Now they are trying to write another plan." This was no more than many other reporters and military analysts were saying. But the airing of Arnett's remarks on Iraqi TV sparked a backlash from critics who said Arnett had played into the hands of Iraqi propagandists. NBC briefly defended him, then fired him.*

*The sensibility Arnett brought to all his assignments was formed during his early years in Vietnam, where he arrived in 1962, a young New Zealander, to work with Malcolm Browne for the Associated Press. He has said that if CNN had covered the war in Vietnam as it covered the war in the Persian Gulf, "the Vietnam War could not have lasted as long as it did."*

———

I remember coming into the bureau [in Saigon] that first day. Mal [Browne] was working hard on a story. He knew I was coming, nodded to me and shook my hand quickly, and went back to the job. I was looking around this small room, and there were various souvenirs. One of them was a water container carved from a large piece of bamboo, which the Vietcong were known to carry into battle. I noticed it was stained with what I presumed was blood. Nearby was what seemed to be a twig, which on closer examination proved to be the skeletal remains of a human hand. Mal later told me he had picked it up in the battlefield just to remind him of what this was all about.

In Saigon we were very, very close to the story. The AP bureau was across the street from the Presidential Palace. Just down the street, you would see heavily manned bunkers of South Vietnamese troops. To be in the Caravelle or the Continental Hotel was to brush shoulders with crew-cut young Americans who may or may not admit to what they were doing there. Military vehicles were all over the place. You would go to a nightclub and there would be South Vietnamese generals partying with their girlfriends. So it was a close-knit environment, and this translated into the way we worked, because you would basically walk out the door and information would be flying toward you.

One of the documents that Mal produced for journalists like myself and others was his assessment of news coverage of South Vietnam, which included practical tips on how to get along in the field. Like, "If you're with the troops, moving through a paddy field, and you hear a shot fired, don't stick your head up to see where it came from, because the next shot will be yours." Like, "Stay away from the radio operator when you're moving through the jungle because they're usually the first hit." He also had assessments of different embassies. The Polish embassy had great vodka but really misleading information. The French would deliberately mislead you over the most superb cuisine. So this was my Bible for years.

The volume of stories that we put out—that AP bureau at the time—was enormous, in working conditions which were most uncomfortable. The air-conditioning in our small office often failed. The bathroom in our first bureau was taken over by the photographers, who turned it into a developing room, so if you wanted to go to the head, you had to walk through coils of drying film. The budget for covering Vietnam in those days was very small.

From the earliest time, in Saigon, there was real competition between the news organizations, and Vietnam was the last great wire service war. In World War II and Korea, the wire services were the main news operations. Their reports were in newspapers all over the world, and they competed fiercely. In Vietnam, AP and UPI were in a competitive stance. So Neil Sheehan of UPI was competing with Malcolm Browne and me. On one level, we would have drinks together and cover events together in the field, and on another, we were passionately engaged in being first with the story and cleverest with the analysis. This basically went right through from my first days in Vietnam to the fall of Saigon in 1975, and we were still fighting to get the story first.

———

*After the assassination of Ngo Dinh Diem by South Vietnamese Army officers in the fall of 1963, there was a period of political chaos, with one coup following another.*

———

The events of 1964 in Saigon were so disastrous in terms of the constant politicking and the coup d'etats that the coverage was never questioned, because the events were worse than the coverage could even portray them, and the risk that South Vietnam could slip very quickly into the hands of the Communists was very clear. The reporting was saying just that, and certainly the Johnson administration had their own agenda for correcting what they saw as a disastrous situation. So for a whole year, we were basically criticism-free.

The pressure on all of us in Saigon began when the first Marine units arrived in Da Nang, and the first stories came out about the difficulties of Marine operations around the Da Nang Air Force base—Marines complaining about their mission. Then, in the first battles, like the Ia Drang Valley, where over three hundred American troops were killed in the most dramatic of circumstances, G.I.s were complaining about the inadequacies of support, or talking about their real fears, or praising the enemy. This led to a whole new barrage of criticism, led by the syndicated columnist Joseph Alsop, who started writing about the inexperience of the reporters in the field, their unpatriotism, their unawareness of the larger issues. The Hearst newspapers questioned our patriotism. Morley Safer and I came under criticism because Morley was a Canadian and I was a New Zealander, so the suggestion was, "How can Canadians and New Zealanders ever understand an anti-Communist crusade?" I wondered at that because New Zealand had contributed two or three thousand troops and artillerymen in the field.

This criticism was aided and abetted by a determined campaign from the Johnson administration, orchestrated to some degree by [press secretary] Bill Moyers in the initial phases, then by Tom Johnson in the later phases—he later came on to run CNN. It was aimed at correcting what they thought was an erroneous image. So how do you correct it? Question the patriotism of the reporters, question their experience, question their judgment. This was with us from 1965 to the fall of Saigon in '75.

———

*The administration's efforts to discredit the Saigon press corps went hand in hand with an elaborate public relations campaign, designed to convince Americans victory was near. In their dealings with the press, Mission officials were directed to exercise "maximum candor and disclosure, consistent with the requirements of security."*

———

Barry Zorthian [a U.S. Foreign Service officer who became chief spokesman for the U.S. Mission in 1964] was a remarkably adept individual, and his job was to improve the image of what America was doing. He introduced phrases like "maximum candor" and had background briefings, all aimed slyly at turning negative information into a more positive spin. I remember he called me up angrily on one occasion and said, "Peter, you've done this whole analysis on where the war is going without even getting a comment from General Westmoreland. We must have our view in your stories. We have the right to have the official view." He didn't like it when I said, "I know as much about this war as General Westmoreland knows." He said, "You can't know as much about this war as General Westmoreland knows." I think history shows that, measuring the two of us, my reports were more accurate than his.

I remember meeting General Westmoreland [in the early 1990s] at a press gathering in Virginia. This is a man who was very critical of my reporting over the years. He said to me, "Peter, you were a good reporter in Vietnam. The one story I could not tolerate is you reporting that I played tennis every morning. I could never forgive you for that." In that story, just a day in the life of Westmoreland, I mentioned that he played tennis. The American public wasn't in the least concerned that the general banged the ball around a little each morning. But the Pentagon and the general himself were really concerned, and he gave up tennis, because he felt it was a negative image.

[The daily press briefing, which reporters called the Five O'Clock Follies,] was one of these events you had to attend because, even though the information was inadequate, there was enough information to make a story. You were stuck with having to do it. Now, because of my seniority at that point—I'd been there three or four years—I was in the fortunate position of not having to cover these briefings. But each time I covered an action in the field, I would return to Saigon and there would be a briefing. And I'd get up and ask a question like: "But what about this, that, and the next thing?" And they would immediately go into a fudge mode. You know, they would start saying that what I was asking didn't really happen, or they would be confusing. They never allowed reality to interfere with information.

The cleverness of the Five O'Clock Follies was they always had enough information to make the lead of the day. Every day the AP and UPI would write a lead on the Vietnam story out of the Five O'Clock Follies. Why? Because they'd talk about air strikes against North Vietnam, body counts, the overall picture. And all of this was unassailable by us. We couldn't cover the war in the north, so if they would talk about steel mills destroyed south of Hanoi, who knew? But it was a headline, right? Or they would come up with a body count: "This week we killed 2,700 Vietcong and North Vietnamese, making a total of 70,000 so far this year." A headline, right? That was why the briefing was so important to American propaganda. That briefing helped sustain the American war effort long beyond the time it should have been sustained.

————

*Arnett was in Saigon in January 1968, when Vietcong forces attacked the capital, and many other cities, during the Vietnamese Lunar New Year celebration known as Tet.*

————

Tet had a major influence on war coverage because suddenly the capital city, where hundreds and hundreds of reporters were based, was under attack, so reporters who spent a lot of time going to the briefings, writing about a war that was some distance from the capital, were suddenly under fire, and the embassy was attacked and the grounds overrun, and dead bodies on the streets, rockets landing on the Continental and Caravelle Hotels. Suddenly all these reporters were war reporters, they were right in the middle of it, and their reporting reflected it. And it did get a lot of focus, and it became controversial—particularly for me because I reported that there were Vietcong inside the embassy. Now, that came from a military policeman who said, "Put your head down, they're firing from the sixth floor." So he's on tape, and that's what he thought. [There hadn't been Vietcong inside the embassy after all, and] we eventually corrected the story. But the administration tried to use that, what turned out to be an error, to sort of protest that all the coverage was wrong.

The Tet Offensive was a complete military surprise. Forty cities and major bases attacked at a time when the U.S. administration said we had the Communists on the run, "we're going to get out of here this year." Complete surprise. Within six months it was clear in all our reporting that the Communists had suffered a huge defeat. There were bodies all over the place, we knew it. But this could not take away from the whole surprise element that the Communist side came up with this incredible deployment of all these forces to shake up the whole U.S. military establishment. That is the story of Tet. The fact that they eventually killed fifty, sixty, one hundred thousand North Vietnamese was not the story, but many historians look back and say tut tut tut, the press missed it. We didn't miss it. We saw it all happening, we reported what was happening. That's what media's meant to do.

You would have hoped that the fall of Saigon would have borne out [the Saigon press corps' early assessments of the flaws in U.S. policy]. You would have hoped that this would dispel criticism. But it didn't do that at all, and it went on, even to today. The press is bearing part of the blame—certainly by right-wing Americans—for losing the war.

From beginning to end in Vietnam, I was never personally concerned about criticism and opposition and the many attempts to muzzle me and others. And I'll tell you why—because I was a field correspondent. I based everything I wrote on being out with the troops. I was in the military operations. I interviewed the generals, the G.I.s. So I knew exactly where I was coming from. I had the quotes. I had the pictures. I was on the side of the angels; I had the information.

My attitude was that my primary role working in Vietnam for the Associated Press was to gather all the relevant information, do my stories, get them back to headquarters in New York, and ultimately they would have to make the decision about using the material. On a couple of occasions they decided not to use controversial stories. By and large, though, they allowed many controversial stories to go through, and they backed us up to the hilt from beginning to end.

If I'd been with, say, the *Washington Post* or the *New York Times,* where they had maybe only one or two reporters, I would have been burdened with doing the analysis, doing the political story, going to the battlefield, going to the diplomatic cocktail parties—basically trying to wrap the whole thing up. Being an AP correspondent, in a team of, say, twenty, I could go out and get the story I wanted. Many of those stories are the ones that raised the hackles of the Pentagon, because I could give details about how soldiers lost their lives, their attitude to the war, their growing discontent. Of course, I also wrote many hero stories. By and large, most of the stories that I and the other reporters wrote were hero stories, because American troops generally fought remarkably well and endured incredibly difficult circumstances.

Take the Ia Drang Valley story, one in which we talked candidly and openly about the bravery of the G.I.s. Sure, there were negatives. They were ill-led at the higher command; there's no doubt about it. The point is that we [at AP] were able to do it. Now, within the whole journalistic community, many journalists couldn't get out to the field, so I had the luxury—some may say, the crazy opportunity—to spend my time with the troops, in the action,

where the blood was flowing, and getting the facts. So many journalists were stuck in Saigon. They were required to be there or
didn't have the desire to spend their time in the field.

What I'm haunted by is the inability of the journalists to get the
story out sooner, that this was the wrong war in the wrong place at
the wrong time. Sure, we challenged authority along the way. We
did brave coverage in the battlefield and came up with the kind of
information that showed early on that this was not worth the price
being paid—the price being sixty thousand American lives, two million Vietnamese lives, billions in capital. We were not able to tell
that story in a way that would convince the U.S. government and
military leaders that this was not worth fighting. That war went on
from 1962, when I first arrived, to 1975, when I left. And my feeling
at the fall of Saigon, when the North Vietnamese tanks rolled in,
was: "What a wasted effort." All those years. All the casualties. All
the enormous effort at nation-building. All of it ended suddenly one
sunny morning, with no real memory of what had gone on, as
though the whole enterprise had been stupid and silly. And at enormous cost to the United States's reputation, plus to so many people.
So I'm haunted by the fact that some of the best reporters in the
whole world couldn't end that long before it should have been
ended.

[In the Persian Gulf War], the pool system came into existence
because it was the only format [under which] the Pentagon would
allow any coverage. From the beginning of the buildup of the coalition in late 1990, when all media organizations in the United
States wanted to be part of this new war, the Pentagon signaled that
access would be absolutely limited, that they were not willing to
allow any kind of extensive coverage, and that the only way was
this pool system. The only access you could have to any units would
be with other colleagues, a limited number, and you would report

back to the rest of the press corps on what you had found, and those reports would be checked out and censored by the military authorities who accompanied the pools. It was unworkable. It was not allowed to work.

The pool system works within the Pentagon, where you have a hard core of journalists who occasionally go on special missions with Pentagon people. It works in the White House, where we have a small pool of reporters who cover the president. Beyond that, it doesn't work, it's never worked, and in the Gulf War it didn't work. It is not the answer to gathering information which the public has the right to know.

When it turned out the pool didn't work—that the military was unwilling to allow the free flow of information, and that it was an inadequate application of all their promises—then you had breakout reporters from the networks and the *New York Times* sneaking around trying to get information themselves, like Bob Simon of CBS and his crew, who were picked up by the Iraqis and imprisoned and their lives were threatened. It's not good for reporters to risk their lives in this way. I don't think reporters should have to risk their lives when the United States or the West is involved in these major military operations. We should be part of the system. In Vietnam, whatever criticisms we had of the military, they allowed us to be part of the system. And not one journalist was killed in Vietnam because he had to go around [press restrictions] to get information. I don't think it should be up to the media to try to outwit our own side in these conflicts. It's too dangerous as it is.

Reporters did not have access to much of the war theater, and therefore Schwarzkopf could lay out his version, the Pentagon's version, the government's version, of day-to-day events, and it was unchallengeable. The media was unable to lay a finger on him, mainly because of some stupid mistakes early on, where some of the younger journalists present asked stupid questions. They were ridiculed. When you had *Saturday Night Live* ridiculing the media, you knew Schwarzkopf had won the war. Schwarzkopf was very cold-blooded about it. He would argue that security was an essential requirement, that he couldn't trust the media in any secure area, and if the media didn't like it they should ask the American public, who supported him fully on that issue. I think he said that on one occasion.

The only fly in the ointment was my reporting from Baghdad, the reporting of CNN from the other side. We could report on, say, the [bombing of a] baby milk plant, allegedly a chemical weapons center. We could report on the air-raid shelter bombed, with hundreds dead.

But Schwarzkopf ruled the roost. He had a unique opportunity and he made the most of it.

I think it's interesting that Schwarzkopf and Colin Powell came out of the Gulf War as the military heroes, and there were no others. Now, in retrospect, as the histories are being written, there were tank commanders and brave soldiers and Special Ops people—you never heard their names. Both Schwarzkopf and Powell went on to make many millions of dollars in speaking fees based on their heroic status. But not one G.I. or one officer other than them is remembered for the Gulf War. No "hometown heroes" [soldiers covered by the media in their hometown]. And during Vietnam there were hundreds of hometown heroes. I know many hundreds of American soldiers who were in Vietnam who have nothing against the media. They treasure the clippings that were in their hometown paper about them. In Kandahar today, in the Special Operations around Kabul and Afghanistan, there is virtually no information, and no hometown heroes.

CNN and live coverage altered forever the way that wars and other crises are covered. For the first time in media history, an event is covered as it unfolds, anywhere in the world. Television news organizations today have the capability of going anywhere and covering anything at any time, and on many occasions they are doing it. It has changed forever the way information is handled. The critics would argue that the traditional gatekeeper role of journalists—to sift through information and present what seems valid in an accurate way—has disappeared with this live coverage. Maybe that's the case. But the point is that the technology does allow information to flow freely. The public is obligated to be more responsible in measuring the impact of information. But that's the way it is, and it's unstoppable.

The Pentagon and the U.S. government [have] every right to present [their] information in any way [they] want to. But the press does have the right to comment, to come up with contrary information, to quote other sources and to have its own reporters around the world, putting their own spin on what's going on. So during the Gulf War, you had Stormin' Norman having a major influence on what Americans were thinking. But you also had Saddam Hussein on CNN for an hour and a half, giving his version of what was happening, and all manner of other people on many other networks contributing to the flow of information.

During my coverage of the bombing of Baghdad and the other cities of Iraq, it became clear to me after two or three weeks that the United States was going after what they call civil military targets, like bridges that weren't used by military traffic. They bombed a bunker. The Pentagon said it was possibly used by senior officials; actually, there were 350 women and children killed. The coverage of that bombing forced the Pentagon to reassess what it was doing in Iraq. They went on to other aspects of the strategic plan that were less detrimental to the civilian public, and still won the war.

You had it in Kosovo, where NATO warplanes bombed the Chinese embassy by mistake. The awareness that that was going on forced Pentagon planners to be more aware. In Afghanistan today, the fact that some villages have been mistakenly hit again forces the Pentagon to rethink its targets, and I think it's a great idea. I think they should. We aren't in the business of blowing away civilians around the world in times of war. Sometimes it happens. But media coverage of these incidents helps military planners keep on track.

If the United States had lost the Gulf War, or if there had been reverses, like chemical weapons killing forty thousand G.I.s, there would have been a different public reaction. All the spin in the world is worthless if you don't have a satisfactory result. The danger in, say, Afghanistan, when information is concealed from the public because the press is being frozen out, is that if there are negative turns in the story, the public will blame the government and the Pentagon, because there'll be no real awareness of what they're doing over there. So I think governments risk a lot if they're not candid. As long as they're successful, the public will go along with it.

Now, the term "partnership" [between government and media] is anathema to many people who feel the press should always be questioning. [But] in terms of national security, a partnership is essential. When the media goes aboard an aircraft carrier, they shouldn't be looking to present information that is negative to the mission. If they go out with an American unit in the field, they shouldn't be looking to provide information that could be detrimental to the safety of those men. To that degree, you're a partnership.

On the other hand, we should also reserve the right to demand accountability from those people who are sending men into action. It works. It has worked in the past. I think it worked in Vietnam. It was the aftermath of Vietnam that gave the press a bad name. It was those who tried to explain away a defeat that used the media as a convenient fall guy.

[During the war against the Taliban in Afghanistan] the U.S. government's overt attempts to control information—not only from

American military sources, but from sources around the world—was overreaching to a ridiculous level. Secretary of State Powell's attempt to have the country of Qatar curtail Al-Jazeera's [the Arabic-language broadcast network] presentations was ludicrous. I have a lot of friends in the Middle East, and they're saying, "Wait a minute. For forty years the United States has preached freedom of expression. Suddenly, we're not meant to have freedom of expression?" And Condoleezza Rice's exhortations to media to be careful of what they put on the air because it undercut national morale—also ludicrous. It reduced the mainstream media to being lackeys of government propaganda.

My approach has always been to start with little points of information and work up. When I was in Afghanistan, at Kandahar Airport, I went to where the 101st Airborne troopers were in their foxholes and I said, "What's happening, guys?" And they told me— occasional sniper fire, this and that, what it was like to live there, what their feeling was about being committed. That to me was a building block toward a broader understanding of what was happening to American troops.

The attack on the World Trade Center was similar to the Tet Offensive in many ways. Saigon was the capital of the Vietnam War; New York is the media capital of the United States and basically of the world. Every journalist in New York that day felt personally threatened by that attack, and all that they've done since reflects that. The press are as mad as hell, as mad as anyone else. They don't like to be hit right in the stomach at home. So the press did not need to be reminded of their national, patriotic duties. They are highly paid to present information in an intelligent and convincing way, and to have the media's judgment questioned was shocking.

The other part of the equation that unnerved me to some degree was the willingness to go along with the idea that only the government knew how to present information. That only the White House knew or could decide what the American public could have or not have. It was silly. Even more ironic, two months later, the U.S. government was showing a bin Laden tape to prove the point that he was involved directly in the World Trade Center, after trying to prevent the showing of tapes earlier that basically said the same thing.

The press has handled dissent [since September 11, 2001] very gingerly. I'm not criticizing it for doing that. I think the media, along with the rest of the U.S. public and much of the world, looked at the terrorist attacks of September 11 as a challenge to our whole concept of stability and our lifestyle. And how to handle any perceived threat to the effort to prevent it happening again was weighed carefully. To this day, the voices opposed to the war on terrorism are not as publicized as they may have been in a previous war. But I find it difficult to criticize the media for that, because we're dealing with pretty visceral emotions here. Having been over to Afghanistan, [I can say that] this is a tough fight. It's dangerous. And I don't know if those who are criticizing policy are fully aware of what it will take in the future to handle this problem.

I personally interviewed bin Laden four and a half years ago. He was a dangerous man then. He remains dangerous today. I wouldn't say for a minute that the press should ignore dissent. But it seems to me this is a time to weigh dissent very carefully.

The American media basically said good-bye to the world in the 1980s, when the bottom line for the print and television media became profit. We had newspapers being sold because they were getting a profit of only 15 percent whereas the owners wanted 30 percent. You had television organizations wanting to increase their bottom line. Even an organization like CNN, after the Gulf War, started reducing staff because they wanted a bigger return on investment.

By ignoring the world, the American public is constantly surprised by developments. Everyone is surprised that India and Pakistan had nuclear weapons. Why? They've been preparing them for years. The public gets surprised at China's occasional assertions of power. They get surprised constantly in the Middle East. Africa is a pit of darkness in the eyes of most Americans. I've looked into this issue, and what it gets down to is editorial decisions. It's newspaper editors and television news directors who make the decisions about what is news and what isn't news. International news is expensive, so newspapers could cut back bureaus overseas and fill up the resulting space with local stories without anyone noticing. Television could do the same thing. Up to the war on terrorism, most of American news management looked at local news as primarily of interest, national news secondary, and international news—you know, forget it.

When you look at the impact on American society, it is enormous. You do have mainstream news organizations like the *New York Times, USA Today,* the *Wall Street Journal,* and the *Los Angeles Times* publishing international news. But they don't reach the mass of American people. The combined circulations of those news organizations are, what? Twenty million max? Where do the other Americans get any information about the world? They don't get it from their local papers. They don't get it from television. They don't get it. That means a government can do pretty much what it wants overseas. But if there are any reverses, there'll be no understanding at home of why those reverses are, and maybe no endurance for the long haul.

FOR FURTHER READING:

Peter Arnett, *Live from the Battlefield: From Vietnam to Baghdad* (Simon and
    Schuster, 1994)

# ┤ CHRIS HEDGES ├

## EL SALVADOR · NICARAGUA · THE MIDDLE EAST
## PERSIAN GULF · THE BALKANS · AFGHANISTAN

*Chris Hedges graduated from Harvard Divinity School in 1979 and became a freelance war correspondent. If that was unusual training, he is an unusual reporter.*

*Hedges wrote mostly about conflicts in Central America and the Middle East before joining the* New York Times *on the eve of the Persian Gulf War. In that conflict, he became well known both for the quality of his coverage and for his defiant independence from the military and his colleagues in the press. He spent several days in the custody of Iraqi authorities. He went on to cover most of the international conflicts of the 1990s.*

*Hedges's views on war, the military, the press, and human nature carry the conviction of a moralist, even of a latter-day prophet. He does*

*not spare himself when enumerating the motives that propel reporters*
*to war. He can seem close to despair. Yet he has said that he views*
*his experiences through the frame of a redemptive faith. Discussing his*
*2002 book,* War Is a Force That Gives Us Meaning, *he told an*
*interviewer: "I try not to use a lot of religious language, but it's there.*
*Sin. Grace. Redemption...I have not found the words that can replace*
*those."*

———

I was a seminarian. I came out of the Social Gospel. My father had
been a veteran of World War II. He was a Presbyterian minister
and a civil rights activist and an antiwar activist, and then ended
his career as a gay rights activist. I had a hard time marrying that
kind of activism to what I saw as the neutral profession of reporting,
but I always wrote. I wrote compulsively, like many writers. I published my first piece in the *Christian Science Monitor* when I was in
college in the late 1970s, early 1980s.

In my mind, Latin America was as close as anyone in my generation was going to come to fighting fascism. I very much wished
that I could have been of [George] Orwell's generation. I went to
Latin America to be a reporter after I finished divinity school, but
only to be a reporter in Latin America. I wasn't interested in rising
within a news organization or going to work for the city desk. So I
ended up in the war in El Salvador as a freelance reporter.

I very much wanted to be like the World War II and Spanish
Civil War generation. Orwell was the big influence on my life, and
then all of the great war reporters. Ernie Pyle, Homer Bigart, A.J.
Liebling [of the *New Yorker*]—these were people that I devoured
and wanted to become. In the case of all those people, [what ap-
pealed to me was their] humanity—that understanding of the pathos
and humanity of war. That's very different from a Drew Middleton
[the longtime military affairs writer for the *New York Times*]. Drew
Middleton was the kind of guy who gave you the big picture, who

sat around and talked to the generals and told you how the battle plan was working out. I was driven to war the same way that Tolstoy was driven to war—that incredibly intimate and horrifying act of killing, of danger, of fear—and that's what these writers all grappled with. I grew up in a small farm town, and this seemed an incredibly exciting and exotic life. It's what I wanted from a very early age.

I think all of us have to shed illusions or myths that we carry into conflicts. I carried them into El Salvador. I mean, I was never a supporter of the FMLN [Farabundo Marti National Liberation Front, the coalition of leftist rebels that fought a twelve-year civil war against the U.S.-backed Salvadoran military], but at the same time, I believed perhaps a more just society could be created through violence. I didn't understand violence. I didn't understand war.

————

*In the Persian Gulf War, Hedges had his first major exposure to a new sort of adversary—a public-relations bureaucracy made up in part of his own colleagues and competitors.*

————

I had just been hired by the *New York Times.* They hired me because I spoke Arabic, I had been in the Middle East, I'd covered conflicts, I'd been in Central America for five years, I'd been in the Middle East for two when they hired me. But they wanted to create a diverse team, and they kept trying to balance it out with the right number of women and the right number of people of color. And because of the fear of gas, nobody wanted to go, and I kept sort of crawling down to the foreign desk on my knees every day, asking if they would send me. Finally, when enough people said they weren't going, two days before we were supposed to leave, they said, "Okay, your number is up. You go." I wasn't prepared, but I went anyway.

I had never covered a conflict in which the U.S. military was directly involved. When we all got off the plane, they handed us a piece of paper that said, in essence, "You'll do everything you're told by the U.S. military, you'll never go anywhere unless we tell you, you'll never report anything..." And it was garbage. It was unbelievable. So I sat in the room and signed it like everyone else, and then promptly ignored it.

The next day I ran into a bunch of friends of mine, all of them of dubious moral character; they worked for tabloids in London, and I'd met a lot of them during the Falklands War, when I was in Buenos Aires. They had gotten a jeep, and they were all going to go up to this town of Khafji [a Saudi Arabian town captured by Iraqi forces, then recaptured], so I went with them. I wrote a story about this abandoned border town; it wasn't a great story, but it had mood and color, and I came back and filed it. It was a complete violation of everything I had signed a few hours before, and was not a pool report, and this immediately started to create problems with my colleagues who were abiding by the rules.

I really didn't come to the Gulf to sit in a hotel and rewrite pool reports. It didn't make any sense to me. It just seemed too humiliating. I mean, I wasn't going to do it. I would rather be thrown out or have the paper send me back [to the United States]. There was some risk, because I was a new employee, but I kept going out. I hooked up with units, mostly the Marine Corps, because the press rules were established by the Army, and the Marines saw this as a great conspiracy against the Marine Corps, and were very welcoming. So I kept filing and filing until the other journalists, who did sit around rewriting the pool reports—or were in the pools, which were very restrictive—sent a letter back to the foreign editor and said I was ruining the *New York Times*'s relationship with the military.

Most of the press welcomed the pool. They wouldn't tell their editors that, but the fact is that in every war I've covered, the number of people who are actually willing to go out—I mean, really go out—is small. Ten, twenty percent, maybe; I mean, it's tiny. Most people want to play war correspondent. They want to sit in the hotel. They may do something mildly daring and then spend weeks talking about it and probably writing about it. But the number of people that really hustle is tiny. So you had that phenomenon coupled with the fact that most news organizations sent people from Washington, and reporters who report out of Washington and reporters like myself, who spend a lifetime in warfare—we hate each other. They make their living by having lunch with policymakers and being on the inside track and being asked their opinion on important world issues, so they can feel like a player, too.

If you look at Washington reporters, after a while they begin to look like congressmen. They survive by building relationships with people who are lying to them. My job as someone overseas is to write: "This is a lie." There becomes a huge antagonism between those of us on the ground and those of us reporting out of Washington, because these guys want to get on the front page, too. The fact that it's mendacious and a bunch of crap is irrelevant. It's been leaked to them; it's an exclusive; and they want it out. This certainly happened in Central America. It happened in Bosnia, and of course during Bosnia you had Dick Holbrooke [U.S. special envoy], who was just the master of this—of deciding who's going to ride in his car and who isn't, who he's going to put on a plane and who he doesn't. You have the press corps reduced to yapping little dogs at the feet of these obnoxious bureaucrats, begging to be included in their entourage. It's absolutely the most bizarre phenomenon. For the fifteen years I've been overseas, it never stopped. The press is very vulnerable to being stroked by the people they should be very critical of. Washington is very, very corrupting, and the longer you do it the more corrupt you become—I'm talking about the press—so these were the people who were sent to the Gulf.

And what did they want to do in the Gulf? They wanted to recreate what they had in Washington. They wanted to be briefed.

They wanted to have background briefings for the big press, like the *New York Times,* which nobody else could come to except maybe the *Washington Post* and CNN. They re-created that whole Washington environment, so that those of us who were actually trying to go out and cover a war free of those restrictions were not only a tiny minority, but were considered a terrible impediment to what they were doing, as well as an embarrassment to themselves because they were getting rockets back [from their editors] asking, "Why didn't you go to Khafji? Why didn't you go here? Why didn't you go there?" So the only reason the pool system worked in the Gulf is because the journalists wanted it to work. The military never could have run that. You had a bunch of self-selected journalists sitting around deciding who was going to go on what pool and it was bizarre.

Of course, I got in terrible trouble and was banned from the hotel by the military and arrested and all sorts of stuff. But after some of my colleagues complained to the foreign desk, I went to Johnny Apple [R. W. Apple, a veteran *Times* reporter and Washington bureau chief], who became my great protector. Johnny called a meeting of all the *New York Times* reporters in Saudi Arabia and said, "Look, we don't work for the U.S. military." Without his protection, I couldn't have continued to work.

The censorship in the Gulf War, in the end, turned against the military. It didn't turn against us [in the press]. The military had essentially a clean war to fight. You can't get more evil than Saddam Hussein. The military itself was well trained. Nobody was taking drugs; everybody had to piss in a bottle every month so everybody was being checked. I mean, it was a pretty impressive force, and they should have let the press loose. But they didn't. The people who devised those press rules devised them for Vietnam. They didn't devise them for the Gulf War.

The military brass in the Gulf War were fighting the press of

Vietnam without realizing that the reporters were not the kind of reporters who were reporting in Vietnam. If you look at that early generation from Vietnam—Halberstam, Mal Browne, others—they went into that conflict believing the military and they got lied to. When I talk to people like Mal, there's still a burning anger, just a deep distrust of the military on every level, and with good reason. My generation [of war correspondents], which essentially was formed in the wars in Latin America, went there very sympathetic to the left, and we were lied to by the left. So the few of us who had actually covered war arrived in the Gulf much more willing to believe the military, because we had been burned by the other side.

[The average soldier in the Gulf War saw the press for] what it was—a giant PR machine for the brass and the Pentagon. They hated the press because of it, and they had every right to. The press was peddling the lies that [General Norman] Schwarzkopf was handing out in the press briefings. For instance, before the war, the Iraqis made this push to take this border town, Khafji—the one I had visited when I first came to the Gulf. The Saudis who were supposed to defend the town hopped in their air-conditioned four-door sedans and got out as fast as they could, and those who didn't have four-door sedans piled into police cars and fire trucks, and the Iraqis walked in without a fight. The Saudis abandoned their town. So the Marines were called in. I was with them. They had to take back the town street by street. In the press briefings down in Dhahran and Riyadh, they stood up and talked about the brave Saudis defending their town. There wasn't a Saudi *in* the town, and the Marines were pissed off. Then, [because of] the few of us who got in there and reported it, they had to amend it and say, "Oh, the Marines helped the Saudis." But the Marines knew it was a lie, like all frontline soldiers know the lies. And there's a lot of anger at the people spinning out the lies, because these guys are putting their lives on the line, and there's a lot of anger at the press who sits there and repackages the lies for public consumption. There was a lot of anger toward CNN during the war.

No war is successfully prosecuted unless it's mythic. You know, we, the good, will triumph because the good always triumph, and the tableau is black and white. World War II was the great myth. Of course, not for the combat veterans. But the press—even Ernie Pyle, who I love—was part of the machine. You fought this black and white battle with evil versus goodness, civilization versus barbarity.

That myth survived the war. There was a huge hangover among many combat vets—the very deep alienation combat vets feel when they enter a society that has believed the myth. That's why combat veterans are so reticent to speak, and when they do struggle to speak, and they write memoirs, they are ignored and shunted aside because people don't want to hear. So we end up pretty effectively silencing the real witnesses we should be listening to.

Why was Vietnam different? The myth broke down. The South Vietnamese government was so unpopular and so corrupt and the lies that Washington and the Pentagon peddled became more and more egregious, larger and larger, so that you couldn't sustain the myth anymore. There was just no reason for us to be there. There was a reason to fight in World War II, and without that reason [in Vietnam] the myth disintegrated.

The Gulf War was a real watershed because it brought back the myth of war. War suddenly became fun again. War became noble again. War became respectable. And that was the great pernicious influence of the Gulf War. The old lie resurrected itself in full glory, and the ghosts of Vietnam were vanquished. We have been living with that lie and exalting war and lying to ourselves about what war is ever since, and we're going to get in really big trouble because of it. In every single war, the press has always been part of the problem. The press has essentially allowed itself to fall into that role of selling the myth. The myth always sells. The myth sells really well. It sells newspapers. Ratings go up. When you *really* report war, it doesn't sell. But as long as you peddle the myth, that's what people want to hear, because you peddle the myth not only about your country, your military, and even yourself, but about us as a people, and people love to hear that. You're stroking a populace. You're talking about how brave they are, how good they are, what courage they have, what they stand for, the forces of light against the forces of darkness, and how we'll all help each other. There's this communal bond, and it has a cultlike quality.

Schwarzkopf, who was this surly, fairly unpopular commander who had been dumped down in Florida because they wanted to get rid of him, suddenly became this cross between Abraham Lincoln and [George] Patton. It didn't matter how unpleasant he was or what new restrictions [were created]. The press couldn't wait to fall all over themselves to do another profile of our leader. It didn't take a brain surgeon to figure out what Schwarzkopf was about, but the press reported myth, and myth sells. Those few people carping around the edges were not listened to, and that's typical. That's what always happens.

I've never seen a reporter endanger the lives of American fighting men. First of all, in the Gulf I had far more combat experience than even the officers. So the notion that I was a danger was garbage. That's not why they're not taking reporters along. That's self-evident.

With every unit I'm with, I expect that in a firefight they will protect me. I do not carry a weapon, and I oftentimes will have bodyguards assigned to me, and I've had situations in firefights where these guys have risked their lives so I can get out. I will never betray the unit I am with. If I'm with the Marines in the Gulf, I will never write anything—their size, their locations, the weapons they're using—anything that in any way will give sustenance to the people opposing them. I would do that if I was on the Iraqi side. I am not a spy. I'm a reporter, and that requires a lot of self-censorship. But based on that premise, I will write the truth without endangering the people I write about. And that is true in every single armed unit I've ever been with. That's my rule.

So much of war reporting is about self-aggrandizement. I'm guilty of that. We all are. "Look at me, the hero. Look at how brave I am. Look at where I went today." Even with the *New York Times,* where you don't write in the first person—that shell that went off twelve feet away, "I was there."

In conflicts where the U.S. military has not been fighting, it's sicker. We become peeping toms of other people's misery. We're riding around a war zone with $5,000 in our pocket—in the old days in a jeep, in the new days an armored car—and it's a great adventure, without any real moral involvement at all.

[Sometimes] we fall into the trap of embracing a cause, of making the Muslim-led government in Sarajevo look like us, or making the Salvadoran guerrillas look like us. They're not us. These movements often don't have our values. Sarajevo remains a city where Serbs and Croats are not welcome. But you would have never known that from the early reporting of the war.

I think a lot of war correspondents are deeply attracted to the military. Look at what they wear—this quasi-military clothing that we all wore, these upgraded Boy Scout uniforms that we cart around from one conflict to another. We're seduced by the power of the machine. We identify with the power of the machine. We get off on it. We like the adrenaline rush. We like the talk. We talk like they talk—people getting "waxed." We fall into the psychosis of war, and it's a sickness, and we're as sick as everyone else. So you ask why we peddle the myth—because the myth promotes us. Because we get off on the myth and because we believe it ennobles us.

A lot of us are very idealistic people, and a lot of our faults come from the fact that we really want to make a difference. I'm not a thrill seeker, at least out of war zones. There has to be a moral component to it. When the Serbs went into Kosovo, and they massacred a bunch of people in a village, and they cut off all the roads and said we couldn't go there, Kurt Schork [a Reuters reporter later killed in Sierra Leone] and I walked. We walked all day long. We got in there and [discovered] that seven people had their throats slit and their village burned. We got the eyewitnesses and walked out and wrote it. I think that is a tremendous service. It made it so much harder for the Serbs to say it didn't happen. You take those risks because you believe there's a moral worth behind it.

Is there a role for good war reporters? Of course, because however much they may buy the myth, eventually, if they are real war reporters, they realize the myth is hollow. Even Ernie Pyle turned, in the end, if you read the last stuff he did. It took him a long time. It's when you finally see it for what it is that you become most effective and most alienated and most depressed. But those finally become great reporters worthy of the profession. I just think there are many that never reach that point.

It's that messianic quality we have that drives our editors nuts, and why, on the one hand, they need us, because we're foolish enough to go do it, and on the other hand why, once we're brought back to the newsroom, we're so unpalatable to this corporate entity. That's been a conflict since this profession began, because those motives that push people like me forward to do these kinds of things are not understood or appreciated or trusted by the news organizations that employ us. They may trust us as reporters, but they don't understand those motives.

There's so much self-censorship that goes on in the press when it comes to transmitting images of violence. That's true in any conflict I've been in. What gets out and is broadcast—whether it's Vietnam or El Salvador or Bosnia or Kosovo—it's so sanitized. It has nothing to do with the reality of what actually took place at the event they're covering. For instance, the Serbs surrounding Sarajevo were firing very, very heavy artillery. And when it comes into a marketplace or a street corner, people are dismembered. People are eviscerated. Half a head is blown off. A stomach is ripped out. People are lying around dying because both their legs aren't there anymore. That's never broadcast. They'll shoot the film, and they'll clean it up and cut it to make it palatable. Now, it will still have tremendous shock value for people who are seeing it, but it doesn't begin to convey the horror of war.

It's true in every war I've covered. Nobody sees war. Editors back in London or Paris or New York don't let anyone see war because it's so horrible. How can you run a video clip of a mother dying, watching the blood spurt out of her arteries? How can you do it? No one ever sees war except the people who are there.

We sanitize war so it makes sense. I mean, war never makes sense. Most of the time in combat you can't figure out what's going on. It's total confusion. You never get that in coverage. Everything has a beginning, a middle, and an end. It doesn't. I've been in fire-fights. I still don't know where they were firing from. It's so horri-fiying. It's so humiliating, because you're so powerless. It's so disturbing. It's so fearful, and you do all sorts of things in fear that you would never expect yourself to do, like hide behind another human being so the bullet will go through them. It's not a conscious decision. In that kind of fright, fear moves you. You don't get any of that [in war coverage]. That's why combat veterans are so reluctant to talk, because it's not a pretty picture, what we do when we're scared.

When I started in this business in El Salvador and Central America, all the networks had correspondents based there. Most of them spoke Spanish—I think all of them. They would go out and do three- to five-minute pieces for the nightly news. Okay, it was only three to five minutes; it tended to be tied to images, and if the correspondent got anywhere near the bang-bang, you can be damn sure that became the story. But you know what? It was a huge step up from what we have now. Now, we have talking heads round the clock with producers standing off on the edge of the rooftop, ripping off or rewriting Reuters or AP copy—because these people don't have any time to report anymore—and having them regurgitate it in long, useless monologues where people are talking about countries and movements and issues they know nothing about. The situation in terms of TV has deteriorated in terms of actual reporting. The fact that the *New York Times* will send a reporter out to a village in Afghanistan to write a story—that doesn't really bother the Pentagon too much. It's the images that bother them.

I don't have a great deal of respect for CNN. I think CNN could have been something, but I think it forfeited that, for whatever reason. It is what it says it is—"Headline News." That's it. It's good for images. CNN brought Christiane Amanpour into Kosovo briefly, but without the backdrop of Sarajevo, it was a story that couldn't fly, that she couldn't sell. It became too hard, and she didn't stay very long.

When I covered Kosovo for the *New York Times,* it was no secret to the editors that very few people were reading my reports. But they believed the story was important, that it should go on the front page, and that it should be given space. And that in the end is what makes the *Times* a great newspaper.

The fact is the *New York Times* and the *Washington Post* are great newspapers. But I do think that there is a difference, finally, between what they do and what I do. They have big corporations to run. I, like many reporters, can carry on my messianic moral crusade, but if the business isn't viable, I'm going to be doing it in my living room. They have to work with the powers that be. I think in the Gulf War, many of the publishers and executives were not as firm as they should have been. That's my feeling. At the same time what they do and what I do are really different, and the reasons we do it are different.

Does the media shape public opinion? Not in war. When everyone's waving a flag, the media waves a flag. When middle-class families start wondering why their boy is coming home in a rubber bag, then the media starts asking questions, too. But not until it's the middle class, because as long as it's poor, black kids, who don't have a voice in our society and with whom the media is pretty far out of touch, those questions aren't asked. In war, the media reacts. It doesn't press forward, except for these tiny exceptions of people who have integrity and are ignored and even reviled for being Communist dupes or for being naive.

I think the really great war correspondents have to accept the fact that ultimately they are ineffective—that the myth will always win, and that they can justify the risks they take and the job they do because they have made a moral choice to do that, and because it is the right thing to do. If they get caught up in trying to be effective, they will give in to despair. They have to measure their moral worth by the fight that they make on a daily basis and the tiny, small, pure victories that they make. The bomb that destroyed this village and these lives and the story you wrote about it. That has to become your victory. In the grand scheme of things, I think, we have to accept a kind of irrelevance.

I think war correspondents all grapple, finally, with war's horror. They may not give it to us completely unvarnished. They may be unable to give it to us without the taint of myth. But in the end, I think, they all become great reporters because they see it for what it is, and they struggle to communicate it within the many restrictions that are imposed upon them, including emotional ones. They rose above the trade to become lights for the rest of us. And that's

why people like me look to them and revere them and st
achieve ultimately what they achieved.

There are always, within the rabble, people who rise
whose voices must always be listened to, however small in number
they are. And I have nothing but unbounded admiration for those
people. A lot of them are dead.

FOR FURTHER READING:

Chris Hedges, *War Is a Force That Gives Us Meaning* (Public Affairs, 2002)

# ⊣ CHRISTIANE AMANPOUR ⊢

PERSIAN GULF · YUGOSLAVIA · SOMALIA
THE MIDDLE EAST · AFGHANISTAN · IRAQ

*It seems likely that no other war correspondent has reported to so many people as Christiane Amanpour. This is due in part to the global reach of the Cable News Network, in part to the multifold violence of her era, and in part to her own apparently tireless affinity for war. Since the early 1990s, Amanpour has been a symbol of television's dominance of journalism, especially of war journalism. If Vietnam was the first televised war, the conflicts of the 1990s and beyond have been packaged into full-blown television productions, and Amanpour is undoubtedly the brightest star of the genre. Yet she has consistently defied her medium's trend toward superficiality and hype. Few if any reporters have paid closer attention to the costs of war among civilians. Her reports from Yugoslavia, for example, will likely endure as leading historical documents of that land's tragedy.*

*Born in London to an Iranian father and an English mother, Amanpour grew up in Iran, attended private school in England, then went to college in the United States. She studied journalism at the University of Rhode Island. She began her career in television as a designer of graphics at WJAR-TV in Providence, Rhode Island, then joined CNN in 1983. She has covered, among many major stories, the breakup of the Soviet Union, the Persian Gulf War, ethnic conflict in the Balkans, the U.S. intervention in Somalia, the Arab-Israeli conflict, and the U.S. war against the Taliban in Afghanistan. In 2003 she returned to the Middle East to cover the U.S.-British invasion of Iraq.*

———

When I first decided that I wanted to be a war correspondent, I didn't have specific role models in view. My experience was a personal one. I had gone through my own war in Iran, the Iranian revolution, and my career, I think, was born out of seeing world-changing, life-changing events at first hand. When I got into this field, and read biographies of the people who went before me, there were obviously key people who stood out. Think of [the Time-Life photographer] Robert Capa, who took those incredible pictures of the D Day landing. Only eleven frames survived, and those are the eleven iconic frames of D Day, and they tell us that whole story. The power of a journalist and of a photographer is remarkable. And then, of course, during Vietnam, the great reporters—David Halberstam, Peter Arnett, Neil Sheehan—all those people, were great inspirations for me. And Walter Cronkite as well, who had such a stellar career. When I knew him he was at the end of his anchor career, but to think what he did in the years before he sat behind that desk is just phenomenal.

• • •

[In the Persian Gulf War,] one thing CNN did was very courageous— and this was [due to] Ted Turner, who is really the last true, courageous, independent news publisher. At a time when all the other major news organizations, particularly the newspapers, decided amongst themselves that they wouldn't be in Baghdad, he said to us, "That's our job. We will be there." But he made it clear that it was voluntary. Whoever wanted to, could, and whoever didn't, didn't.

CNN was everywhere. We were in Baghdad. We were in Israel. We were in the Arab countries. We were in Saudi Arabia and then in Kuwait. So we would get it from all sides. The foreign press would tell us we were too pro-American. The Americans would tell us we were too pro-Iraqi. We came under huge criticism [in the United States] from whatever you want to call it—the right wing, whichever wing—for giving succor to the enemy. I think this was unfair. You could criticize the tone. You could criticize maybe a couple of words here and there. But I believe we did a great service by being on that side and by being on every side, in terms of coverage and where we were. I think CNN got it about right, maybe by default.

What CNN did just by being there in the Gulf War was electrifying. I don't think anybody will ever forget where they were the night the bombs started falling over Baghdad. They'll never forget that unbelievable reportage from the three correspondents we had in the hotel there, and those pictures—the night-scope pictures of the antiaircraft fire and the noises and the explosions. For the first time, we were behind so-called enemy lines, and we were able to transmit what was going on. So this was a revolution.

Since then, we and others have tried to repeat that, so that every war now becomes a night-scope, grainy-coverage kind of war— people trying to get the bombs as they fall—dramatic, first-person sort of reportage. That's good and bad. The good thing about it is that it opens up another avenue that often before was closed. I think twenty-four-hour coverage also has had some negative aspects, because it puts undue pressure on policymakers. It forces people to react immediately rather than with consideration.

For instance, when we showed pictures in Somalia of that one American soldier who was dragged through the streets, over and over and over again. In a young Clinton administration, it had a very bad impact. It caused President Clinton, under pressure, to end the mission, and that had a terrible, terrible impact on what the administration did or did not do in Bosnia and other engagements during the 1990s. I think that while there is so much we can offer by good and responsible television reportage, we have a responsiblity about just how we play things.

By bowing to the Pentagon's desire to control the image in the Gulf War, we presented war as a risk-free, casualty-free operation, as a surgical operation. It was a lie. There's no such thing as a casualty-free war. I think that had the effect of preventing the [Clinton] administration from doing what it should have done in Bosnia and in Rwanda, and that was to intervene early. They didn't until it was too late. I think the idea that unpalatable, unpleasant pictures would turn up on television prevented the administration from taking action that could have saved hundreds of thousands of lives. I regret that very deeply, because in the end, we have a responsibility, and in the end, what we did or didn't do had a direct bearing on people's lives. It's really as powerful and dramatic as that.

I do take some comfort in the fact that they intervened in Kosovo early. They saved hundreds of thousands of lives in Kosovo. I think they didn't want to see the images of suffering people, so we had a good effect there.

During the Gulf War, when this draconian new philosophy of censorship came in, suddenly we found ourselves in these pools. Now, I had been covering the whole buildup, ever since Saddam Hussein invaded Kuwait [in 1990], so I really hoped to be able to cover the war as well. Instead, like in roulette, we were picked and put into pools. My pool was on an aircraft carrier in the Red Sea, about as far away from the battlefield as you can imagine. Nonetheless, I said, "We'll do it. It's going to be interesting. At least we'll have one angle of it." We got there the night before the war started, and at a certain time, the admiral said [over loudspeakers], "Men, we have been given the order to strike deep inside Iraq. You've trained well. Good hunting and godspeed and return safe." It was electrifying. Of course, we knew we couldn't break that secret because it wasn't going to happen for several hours hence. But then we started to try to talk to aircraft pilots and various people as the days went on, and we were prevented from asking them specific questions—anything meaningful. So we started to just do color [feature stories]. One of my colleagues had been in a recreation room with the fighter pilots when they came back, and he had written in his copy that they were laughing, chatting, talking, reading between air strikes, and that some of them were reading girlie magazines. This is not an issue of national security. They censored it. Now, that is an example of censorship purely for image. It's got nothing to do with anything military, and I found that far beyond the rules.

I don't think we [correspondents] bear responsibility for the failure of the pool system. I think the pool system itself was a failure. I think we bear some responsibility for the failure to report the war in full. I think we reported it as accurately as we could have done, but lost a lot of texture. We on the ground pushed very, very hard. Many of my colleagues went around the system, with certain dangerous results. [CBS News correspondent] Bob Simon and his crew were captured for wandering into Iraq and spent the entire war in Iraqi jails. This had a chilling effect, as you can imagine, on many people. In my view, the restrictions that the Pentagon put on us forced some of us to break rules and do things that maybe we wouldn't have done had we had normal access.

I think our bosses bear a lot of responsibility, because they are the people who made the deal with the Pentagon. Walter Cronkite said to me he's just amazed that every single day the executives of our networks and our newspapers are not pounding on the doors of the Pentagon and demanding access. I think that is their role. It's got nothing to do with profits.

I have always got on very well with the commanders, with the soldiers on the ground. There's an element of respect, of "We've seen each other before." People get to know which reporters they can trust. When it comes to the public information officers, their brief is from the political side, for the most part. They are concerned 95 percent with image. That's where the balance gets out of whack. That's where we start facing problems as to whether we are being censored and denied access. [Is it] for legitimate reasons of security, or is it because they want things to look a certain way? Increasingly, the balance is too much in favor of controlling image and not security. The more there is of twenty-four-hour news coverage, the more there is a globalized TV environment, the more that people are going to want to control that image. I think it has a net negative effect on what viewers get. Viewers are poorer when we journalists are not able to bring them full, accurate, proper stories in all their aspects, military and human.

There always is a balance between what the military wants and needs and is entitled to, and what we, as journalists in a free society, are also entitled to. With the American military in Afghanistan, the balance is completely out of whack. The politicos in the Pentagon have decided that less is more, that they simply don't want to see too much coverage of the military operation unless it's 100 percent controlled by them. I think that does a great disservice. While we fully accept legitimate reasons for restrictions and censorship—and there are legitimate reasons in wartime—I and many people do not accept being handcuffed and restricted when you are covering ordinary or even extraordinary military operations.

There are understandings that responsible journalists can have with the powers that be. Many of us reporters have been in the field much longer, have covered many more wars, have been on many more fronts, than some of the [military] people in the field. We know what we are doing, and many of us have a deep sense of responsibility. But our primary motive is to cover the operations and bring the story back.

American soldiers fight on behalf of the citizens of the United States. I think it is wrong to suggest that those citizens don't have a right to know what their people are doing. The military in the field are proud of what they are doing and want to get their story out, want their friends and family and the rest of the world to see what they are doing.

We have gotten a very empty view of what is happening in Afghanistan, and it is a dangerous view, because you get the impression that all America is about is bombing and high tech and bulldozing. I think America needs to have its other side shown to the world—its human side, the good things, the constructive things it is doing. By denying us access, I think the military is damaging the reputation of the United States.

The news briefing has become the news even more so after the Gulf War. Any time there is a press conference, television stations take it live, whether it is at the White House, the State Department, in a battle zone, a command headquarters—it's become part of what fills twenty-four-hour news. The latest incarnation of that has become the Rumsfeld Follies. [U.S. Secretary of Defense Donald] Rumsfeld became the voice, the image, the public face of the war against terror, particularly in the initial months [after the terrorist attacks of September 11, 2001]. That was sometimes good, sometimes amusing, and sometimes it backfired. He could make many comments that were funny, [but others were] very unfeeling—and remember, news is now being broadcast to an audience that is not just sitting in front of you, or even in your own country, but around the world. So what you say now, live on CNN or any of the other global news organizations, has consequences way beyond what you say to the group of people in front of you.

Look, let's be very frank. The television news business has become a caricature of itself, and therefore has become the butt of jokes. It has become a *sport du jour* to make fun of television. There's nothing we can do about it. At the beginning of the Afghan War, there were umpteen stories—you can't imagine how many reporters were covering reporters. We were all being asked questions by fellow reporters for different feature stories about covering the war, and they were all just ripping us to shreds for trying to do our job. What can you do?

On the one hand, twenty-four-hour satellite television news has done so much to open up the world, to democratize information, to make sure that no evil dictator can do what he wants to do in secret. But for journalists it becomes even more dangerous than it was before. The targets of our reporting are watching and listening to us on a real-time basis, so we are directly in the line of danger from the people who just want to shut us up.

————

*After the terror attacks on the United States in 2001, high officials in the Bush administration cautioned broadcasters about airing videotapes of Osama bin Laden, and some media executives seemed willing to skew coverage of the war in Afghanistan in the name of national security. For a time, it appeared that journalists were under pressure to curtail their traditional commitment to reporting the news freely.*

————

A lot of things happened in the post–September 11 environment that shouldn't have happened, that perhaps, with cooler heads, we would have stood firmer against. But I think you can understand that. I think America was really traumatized. For the first time in its history, it had been attacked on its soil, and in the most unimaginable manner. To this day, I find it hard to believe what happened. [It was] truly abominable. So the media of the country felt its position was to be patriotic, to rally around the commander in chief, to do what it saw the people of the country doing—partly following the lead of the people and partly because they are Americans themselves. This was their country that was being attacked, and natural instincts came out.

I think that you probably would not find many people defending those decisions in retrospect. [It was] outrageous—taking an order from the White House not to play tapes [of Osama bin Laden]; issuing orders about how to say things on television, what to say, how to caution people about political viewpoints—something we wouldn't accept in normal environments. I think if you were to ask the decision makers, they would agree with you, in retrospect, that those decisions were born out of an unparalleled sense of attack and endangerment.

I believe the press has played a role [in the demonization of enemies], but I think it is usually in the beginning of a conflict, when everybody's emotions are raw. As things settle down, as we get into a rhythm, as we've been at a location for a certain period of time, as this goes on longer than a day or a week or a month, then I think demonizing starts being less of a problem.

We in the press have been accused, often unfairly, of creating and influencing policy. This accusation was lobbed a lot during the Balkan War. My honest opinion is that we do have an effect, sometimes negative and sometimes positive, but we cannot make policy unless there is a policy vacuum. As long as an administration does not have a coherent policy, then that vacuum will be filled by television pictures or newspaper stories or radio reports. But as long as they have a policy, then I think our influence is the right one. We're able to bring [to viewers and readers] the reality of what's going on—the humanitarian situation, the political situation, the military situation.

After September 11, many people in the United States started asking, "Why? What happened? Why did these people hate us? What is the reason for this?" There's no real explanation for what these maniacal suicide bombers did, other than they hate the United States. But there's a lot of context we can tell people about why the United States is viewed in a certain way, particularly in the Muslim world. We reporters following the international world tried to provide that context, and some of us were roundly criticized for doing so, as if we had no right to explain what was going on in the rest the world.

It is the businesspeople, the bosses who are in charge of our organizations, who have decided—for commercial reasons, mostly—that Americans don't need to know about international news, that they don't need to know anything other than business news, tabloid trivia, titillating stuff. September 11—I believe, I hope—changed that for good. It certainly changed it immediately, but I hope it changed it for good, forever. [The attacks] just showed how much—for their own security, if for nothing else—Americans must know about what is going on beyond the shores of the United States. I have always believed that Americans *do* care and *are* interested, as long as stories are told in a compelling and relevant manner, as long as the storytellers are interesting. People want to know what is going on, but our corporations have relied on what I call "hocus pocus focus groups" that tell them essentially what they want to hear and fits their business plan. The net result is you get to a situation like September 11 and the whole country is saying, "Why didn't we know more about this? Why didn't you ever tell us?"

. . .

I've always had one goal in mind, and it's not the trite goal of "the people's right to know." I really believe, from the bottom of my heart, that many of the stories that I am assigned to cover are of vital importance. And without that kind of information, people are simply poorer off. They don't have valuable nuggets that may one day provide for their own security on a very basic level. I've always tried to report the human side of whatever I'm reporting, whether it's a famine or a war or a political crisis, not just to be wrapped up in high-tech gadgets and gizmos. I've always tried to [show] how it affects ordinary men, women, and children.

If you didn't have an independent and free press, you'd have propaganda—ours, theirs, whoever's. You need a free press to sift through the propaganda and tell the story of what's going on, whether it's going well or badly. We are the brokers of information, and if we don't exist, a nation, a civil society, a democracy is poorer. So many countries I have traveled in and worked in do not have a free press, and they are poorer. I'm not saying that every journalist is a great, shining example to mankind. That's definitely not the case. But I think the job of a journalist is a very noble one.

The great Katharine Graham [the late publisher of the *Washington Post*] once said—I'm probably going to misquote her, but to paraphrase it: "What is the good of having this great platform if you can't do something with it?" What's the point of having all this money, all this power, if you can't do something with it? That's the balance that the proprietors have to get right. Obviously, it is a business, but if it is just a business, at the expense of doing good journalism, then we are nothing and we should be run out of town. If you can use your prestige, your power, your money to do good journalism, then I think you should be proud.

## ═══┤ EPILOGUE ├═══

## THE WAR IN IRAQ, 2003

*A new chapter in the history of war correspondence was written early in 2003, when the United States attacked and overthrew the Iraqi regime of Saddam Hussein. As the Bush administration prepared for war, the U.S. Department of Defense announced that print and broadcast reporters would be "embedded" with particular units throughout the armed services. The policy would not afford reporters the freedom to shift between units that their predecessors had enjoyed in World War II and the war in Vietnam. But it offered far better access to the battlefield and to fighting troops than reporters had been allowed in the conflict in Panama or the first Persian Gulf War. Hundreds of journalists signed up to become "embeds"; the Pentagon was hailed for a new openness; and for several weeks, journalists filled American news-*

*papers and broadcasts with words and images from the war zone. Most of the coverage originated from embeds. Some of it came from reporters known as "unilaterals," who worked without being embedded in particular units. More than a dozen journalists lost their lives in the war.*

*In May 2003, about a month after the main fighting ended, four of the veteran journalists who took part in the* Reporting America at War *project offered their opinions of the coverage of the war in Iraq. They were Malcolm Browne; Gloria Emerson; Ward Just; and Christiane Amanpour, who covered the war for CNN. Amanpour split her time between the two modes of reporting. At first she was embedded with a British unit, the Royal Marine Commandos, in the Basra region; then she went to Baghdad as a unilateral. Browne and Emerson followed the news from their homes in the United States. Just watched most of the war from France.*

———

MALCOLM BROWNE: I think that the Pentagon pulled a very smooth one with the American people and the press in particular. I think it was a change of tactics. The Pentagon had come to realize that direct confrontation with the press is counterproductive in many ways, and it's much better to appear to be highly cooperative than otherwise. That way at least you stand a chance of not being criticized so much. The embedding process itself was so smooth and happy that I think the reporters involved never quite realized what a suppository it was. That may not be entirely fair. It was certainly a sea change. But there was no real change in Pentagon attitudes toward the press. I have always felt that the wounds inflicted by the military on the press and vice versa during the Vietnam War have never been forgotten or forgiven. Despite how smooth everything seems to be at the moment, it's a superficially happy situation. I think it isn't real.

General William Tecumseh Sherman in the Civil War perhaps best expressed the perennial attitude of the military [toward the press]. His most famous quote was that if Napoleon had had a war correspondent with him, he would have lost all his battles.

CHRISTIANE AMANPOUR: On the whole, [embedding] provided very good television but not great journalism. Television is all about visuals and images, and the embedding process provided quite a lot of that. But it was such a narrow, narrow slice of what was going on. Each embed, and each unit, really, was completely self-contained. They didn't know the big picture. They didn't know what else was going on in the rest of the battlefield. So there was no big-picture reporting that came out of the embedded reporters.

That's why, in the end, I preferred my own experience, which was sort of a hybrid between being embedded and going unilateral. I felt that I got all the advantages of seeing the military units close up—and also being with the British headquarters unit I was with. The British were much more prone to give detailed briefings to the correspondents who were with them. I got very good big-picture briefings.

[Embedding] is just another pool. It's just called by a different term. What are pools? Pools are controlled and supervised methods of reporting. Now, in previous instances, the pools meant a small and restricted group of people. In this instance, it's meant a massive group of people. Nonetheless, they're still operating under varying degrees of restriction. Now, many of the reporters will say, and I believe them, that they got very good, close-up, honest access to the people they were with. But the fact of the matter is that they didn't get the whole picture. Nobody's going to get the whole picture all the time. But what did we see and what did we get? Very good, dramatic coverage, but also a big lack of [reporting] of what happened to the other side.

There's just one problem with the unilateral situation, and that is that it's very dangerous, especially in wars that are so high-tech and rapid, such as this last one was.

WARD JUST: If you want to compare it to Vietnam, those of us who were out there were, in effect, embeds, with this one difference. You were embedded for anywhere from twenty-four to seventy-two hours, sometimes four or five days, and then you'd go back—I'm talking about print, not so much TV—and you would write an account of three days' action. You'd stay in Saigon for a week and then you'd go out again. And each time you went back, you brought with you all the baggage from the previous encounters. So, finally, after you were there for six or seven months, you had a pretty good idea of tactics and strategy. As a consequence, your correspondence got stronger the longer you were there, and you were able to take what might have been an ordinary firefight in some nameless village and make something out of it, because you came to know what the mission really was and what constituted the fulfillment of the mission. You didn't always know that right away when you started out. Everything in this world takes some experience, and that did, too. It was sort of like serial marriage. These guys [in Iraq] didn't have the opportunity for that. All they saw was the Humvee or the tank.

MALCOLM BROWNE: It's all very well to say embedding brings you close to the marrow of combat, brings you close to the soldiers themselves, and gives you the feel of the situation. But I think there's a tremendous price to be paid. Getting too close to your subjects in your reporting can be very undesirable in some respects, and I think there was certainly some of that.

Embedding seems to me an imitation in some respects of the German system in World War II, in which the propaganda ministry assigned specific reporters and photographers to go to specific battlefields. The German Army looked after them very well. They had access to any kind of transportation they wanted. They could go anywhere. They could do practically anything. The only thing was they were under strict censorship by the Goebbels [propaganda] regime, and it was only after the war that some of the very good coverage that had resulted on the German side came to light.

I think that the embedding process in Iraq is a little bit reminiscent of [the German experience] in the sense that: "We'll give you anything, provided you write what we want." And the temptation to do that is, I think, quite strong.

I think the metaphor of looking at the war through a soda straw many times over is an apt one [for the coverage that resulted from embedding]. The thing that was most singularly lacking in the coverage, I think, was the overview perspective. The political aspect was perhaps underplayed in favor of the most dramatic battle scenes. Obviously television is after the most dramatic possible pictures they can get, and nothing is more dramatic than battle or dying people or miserable people or looting people—the sort of thing that is synonymous with action movies these days. But there's always something missing when you concentrate so fully on action—the exhaustion and the seething hatred that may have taken generations to build up, all sorts of subtleties that are missed in the heat of battle. I listened to BBC and National Public Radio a good deal, and I think they examined the issues in depth more than the networks.

―――

*Ward Just was in France during most of the Iraq War. He followed events in English-language newspapers and on CNN, the BBC, and the French television network Antenne 2, which carried a good deal of coverage from Al-Jazeera, the Arabic-language network.*

―――

WARD JUST: [Television coverage] seemed to me to be startlingly incoherent. The process of embedding probably is not an inherently bad practice. But as a practical matter, what you see is one fragment after another. They didn't tell you very much. You know, little rockets going off in the background, and the correspondent is whispering into the radio camera, and there's a Humvee in the background and a couple of tanks, and sometimes they're firing, and sometimes they're not, and it didn't add up to very much. So toward the end of March, my wife and I basically stopped watching.

We found Antenne 2 more interesting, because it was showing a lot of Al-Jazeera stuff. The images were arresting, and, of course, it was being told from the point of view not of the doers, but of the done to, which is quite another way to go about it. You were looking at it from the other side of the line, which I found to be interesting, and I thought the camera work, for the most part, was very good. They would present a coherent story with a beginning, a middle, and an end. It was a story with a particular point of view, but I wasn't born yesterday. I can figure that out.

GLORIA EMERSON: The most remarkable piece of all the reporting done in the Iraq invasion, a small masterpiece, was by Peter Maas in the *New York Times Magazine*, April 20, 2003. The piece is called "Good Kills." Maas was embedded with the Third Battalion, Fourth Marines. Everything is in this piece: an American Marine sniper from Vermont who is dying; Iraqis trying to flee Baghdad who were killed by the Marines because in all the noise of war, they did not understand the warning shots; and the Marine colonel who said: "It's smashmouth tactics. There is no sense in trying to refine it. The crueler it is, the sooner it's over. We'd like to think of American troops as merciful and nice. They aren't. Soldiers never are."

The best film I saw was on CNN. It showed Iraqi men trying to squeeze and claw their way into buildings where they felt their relatives had been imprisoned. Their faces were desperate. But there was no one in the buildings to liberate.

There wasn't much to film, was there? [Reporters] were usually quite far from the fighting. So what you would see is a correspondent saying, "That's artillery over on that ridge line." I mean, it wasn't Morley Safer at Cam Ne. It was all quite remote.

Print reporters came out much better than television reporters. John Burns of the *New York Times* and Anthony Shadid [of the *Washington Post*], both in Baghdad, did an excellent job. I watched a lot of television but don't remember any of it except for the Abrams tanks and the armored assault vehicles. I wish someone had embedded themselves in a Baghdad hospital during the bombing, then written a piece about what that was like.

WARD JUST: I think that newspaper reporters have somehow neglected the gift of sheer descriptive prose, and along with that, an ear for dialogue—not so much the interview you're conducting but the stuff that's overheard, that, if you choose the right bits, can be tremendously revealing about the atmosphere of a particular action. I found the material that I was reading often quite dry, and I didn't feel I was there. I'm not talking now about the news analysis and the overview, but for a particular kind of war correspondence, if you find yourself in a particularly violent action, I think you want to put the reader there. You want to show them how this man died, and how that man died, and what the objective was, and how you moved toward the objective. In a battle of fire and maneuver, you want to describe both the fire and the maneuver.

Their descriptive gifts seemed to me to be lacking. I'd read this stuff and I'd know at the end of it they went so many miles and killed this or didn't kill that, but I just did not feel inside the tank or inside the Humvee or inside the tent.

I put this thought to a friend of mine who's in the business, and he thought it's because the print reporters take too much account of television. They think television provides the description, and if they did that, they would be duplicating television. [They feel] they've got to bring something else to it—a sense of analysis—

because TV has all the bombs bursting in air on the box, and the viewer can see it. But I think anybody who's ever spent any time in a war knows perfectly well that a battle dispatch, if it's well written enough, will trump a film any time. I believe that absolutely.

———

*After the war, some reporters said they worried that the embedding program had caused them to identify too closely with the units they were covering, thus compromising their ability to report the war dispassionately.*

———

WARD JUST: I don't understand those complaints. You're just a reporter; you're not seeing these things with the eyes of God. You've just got your own two eyes and whatever baggage you're bringing. I think it's a bit naive and, frankly, beside the point. If by embedding you can really have an understanding of the personalities at work and the various capabilities of the commander of the unit, the deputy commander, the scouts and so forth, and have a sense of how the unit is operating as a unit, it seems to me that for war correspondents this is invaluable. You can watch it almost like an organism under a microscope, and you've got to be there a while before you can see that. That's tremendously valuable for the work that you're doing, for the stuff that appears on the page at the end of the day.

AFTERWORD

As I went through these interviews in the late winter of 2003, a
friend of mine was getting ready to accompany U.S. troops into Iraq.
One night an e-mail came from his wife. "I'm afraid John's comfy
days in Kuwait City are now over," she told us. "As of today, he is
officially embedded with the Marines."

I knew John wouldn't have much time to read. But I wondered
which sections of these interviews I ought to clip and send to him
in e-mail bundles from home. But then his wife said there was sand
in his laptop, so he probably couldn't receive any more e-mail
anyway.

Should I have sent him Walter Cronkite, saying war correspondents are essential to democracy? Or Chris Hedges, warning about
the insidious chumminess of the Washington reporters and the military? Or David Halberstam's injunction to search for "the cutting
edge" of the story? Should I have sent him the column Ernie Pyle's

editors didn't publish, even after he was killed—the one about "the unnatural sight of cold dead men scattered over the hillsides . . . dead men in such familiar promiscuity that they become monotonous"?

All these things would have been good for him to read. But what John really needed was the support of his editors and his newspaper—especially the assurance that if he did excellent work, he would have plenty of space in the paper to tell his stories. Good reporters need more than a few column inches. Probably the editors should have sent John to that distant place three years ago, or five, to ask questions that might have helped us to avoid the war in Iraq, or at least to understand it better when it came. But the editors didn't send him in 1998. They would have thought no one cared.

Malcolm Browne speaks here of the ABC News president who told him, in 1965, that television was a medium of entertainment, even when it came to news—that news, in fact, was put on television only because federal regulations required it. Otherwise, the executive told Browne, the networks would replace news with "grade Z westerns and do fine."

Anyone who values good journalism will cringe at this, because it seems to be an abdication of responsibility. But the ABC man was probably right about what the public wants. If no one is listening, you can't blame the news media for deciding to talk about something else. The First Amendment was written to protect the press not for its own good, but for the good of the public. We bear the ultimate responsibility for the quality of our journalism. We are the market for good journalism, and if we ask editors and broadcasters for it, we will get it. If we choose not to care about the world until the world comes crashing through our door, then we will not get it. Not at all, or only when it's too late.

*James Tobin*

## ACKNOWLEDGMENTS

This book, and the documentary film series from which it sprang, began as so many things do nowadays—with a random encounter on the Internet. Intrigued by a Website devoted to the Writing 69th—created by a passionate amateur historian named Jim Hamilton—my longtime collaborator, Michelle Ferrari, and I set out to produce a documentary film that chronicled the history of American war correspondence. To say that the subject was vastly more complex than we initially realized would be an understatement; and were it not for the dedication and insight of our colleagues, as well as the invaluable assistance of the project's many friends, *Reporting America at War* would likely never have come to fruition. It is my great pleasure to thank them here.

My gratitude goes first to the extraordinary team at Insignia Films: Producer Amanda Pollak, whose clarity, professionalism, and unfailingly calm demeanor contributed immeasurably to every conceivable aspect of the production; Associate Producer Cornelia Calder, who oversaw the massive task of conducting visual research for both the film and the book with her characteristic tenacity, impeccable organization, and almost unfathomable good cheer; the series' film editors, Toby Shimin and George O'Donnell, whose dogged attention to detail and keen creative insights influenced the shape and tone of the film profoundly; their assistants, Ryan Widmer, Don Bernier, and Beth Poague, who met the day-to-day challenges and impossible deadlines in our crowded editing room with unflagging energy and efficiency; and finally, Production Associate Ben Ostrower, who managed to juggle last-minute research requests, technical triage, and overall office management with admirable aplomb.

Our skilled cinematographers, Buddy Squires, Allan Palmer, Peter Nelson, Terry Hopkins, and Gary Grieg, gave the film its distinctive look, and the prodigious talents of our composer, Joel Goodman, and our narrator, Linda Hunt, combined to lend texture and resonance to our soundtrack. We owe a similar debt of gratitude to the panel of advisers who shared their extensive knowledge with us and guided the development of the series from conception to completion, among them William Hammond, Larry Lichty, William Leuchtenberg, Rick MacArthur, Don North, and James Tobin. Another set of advisers provided critical help in our fundraising and early script efforts, including Nancy Sorel, Ben Bagdikian, and Roger Spiller. Max Rudin, publisher of the essential *Reporting World War II* and *Reporting Vietnam*, offered vital encouragement and perspective in the project's infancy; without him, the film might never have gotten off the ground. And a special thanks to advisers Alan Brinkley and Geoffery C. Ward, whose insightful critiques and suggestions strengthened the series' narrative considerably.

*Reporting America at War* would not have been possible without the generous support of the National Endowment for the Humanities, the Corporation for Public Broadcasting, the Public Broadcasting Service, Dr. Jonathan T. Howe of the Arthur Vining Davis

Foundations, and our coproduction partner and presenting station to the PBS system, WETA-TV, in Washington. We are especially grateful to Karen Fuglie Miles, our program officer at the NEH, for her patience and encouragement during the project's fundraising phase; to Sandy Heberer, John Wilson, and Steven Gray of PBS for their steadfast faith in the project; and to Dalton Delan and David Thompson of WETA, whose tireless championing of the series has, at various points, literally kept us afloat. Our thanks also to our gifted legal and accounting team of Jim Kendrick, Ed Weisel, and Andrew Hall, who together made certain we had the rights and resources to get the film in the can.

The publication of this book owes much to Peter Kaufman of IntelligentTelevision, who tracked us down early in the project and persuaded us to create a companion volume to the film series. It is thanks to his foresight and perseverance—not to mention his utterly irreplaceable sense of humor—that this volume exists. Series adviser James Tobin graciously took on the book at the eleventh hour and single-handedly transformed our raw interview transcripts into elegant and informative prose—an accomplishment for which we are eternally grateful. Our thanks also to our publishers at Hyperion for their interest and support, and especially to our editor, Mark Chait, whose enthusiasm for this project has been nothing less than infectious.

Finally, I would like to thank the many talented correspondents who agreed to share their experiences with us, both on camera and within this volume; the board of directors of Insignia Films—Daniel Esty, David O. Ives, John Sughrue, and Robert A. Wilson—who have provided wise counsel during the five years it took to bring this series to the screen; and Anne Cleves Symmes, without whose support this project would not have existed at all.

*Stephen Ives*
*Garrison, New York*
*2003*

# INDEX